FAST FOOD — REAL FOOD

Don't worry if you don't feel like cooking. You can eat healthily and provide for a family without the slightest tinge of guilt, without spending hours over a hot stove. This book shows you how.

FAST FOOD
REAL FOOD

Healthy and enjoyable meals — on the table within ten to thirty minutes

Edited by

MIRIAM POLUNIN

Photography by John Welburn Associates
Cover photography by Paul Turner
Illustrated by Clive Birch

All the recipes in this book have been
tried and tested by the *Here's Health* Cookery Team
Those contributed by readers are acknowledged in the text.

THORSONS
THORSONS PUBLISHERS LIMITED
Wellingborough, Northamptonshire

NEWMAN TURNER PUBLICATIONS LIMITED
West Byfleet, Surrey

First published May 1983
Second Impression May 1983

British Library Cataloguing in Publication Data

Polunin, Miriam
   Fast food — real food.
   1. Cookery
   I. Title
   641.5'55   TX652

   ISBN 0-7225-0863-8
   ISBN 0-7225-0817-4 Pbk

Printed and bound in Great Britain

CONTENTS

Dedication

The editor would like to thank Archie Peat
— for help with love.

We gratefully acknowledge the assistance of Harrods and Fortnum and Masons in supplying cookware and stationery for the illustrations in this book.

INTRODUCTION
About These Recipes

We have chosen recipes with a low-fat content, and suggest that you use a measure to count out oil and fat, to preserve this important feature. As the ingredients are unrefined — so that they will retain the maximum food value — and include mainly foods from the plant world, most of the recipes have a good fibre content which is much better than adding bran to refined meals.

Occasional recipes are relatively high in fat — either because they are based on a natural high-oil ingredient, like sesame seeds, or because a certain level of fat is necessary for the recipe to work. These recipes are marked with this symbol ★. Fish recipes and a few others are low in fibre, and marked with this sign ✔.

Measurements

American cup measurements are given for all the recipes. English cooks may also like to measure in cups, if you find it more convenient. To do so, find a mug that has straight sides and buy an indelible china marker pen. Weigh out 8 fl oz of water on an ordinary scale, and pour into the mug. Where it comes to is 1 cupful (US measure). Then mark quarter and half cup measures in the same way. For many recipes, measurements are not critical, but for baking, especially items such as brandy snaps or choux pastry, we do think weighing is more accurate.

Measuring spoons of 15ml (1 tablespoon), 5ml (1 teaspoon), and 2.5ml (½ teaspoon) are used throughout.

American tablespoons are slightly smaller than UK ones, and this has been allowed for. The American pint contains 16 fl oz, compared with the UK 20 fl oz pint.

Oven Temperatures

Electric °F	Electric $_l$°C	Gas	
225 - 250	110 - 130	¼ - ½	Very cool
275 - 300	140 - 150	1 - 2	Cool
325	170	3	Warm
350	180	4	Moderate
375 - 400	190 - 200	5 - 6	Hot
425	220	7	Very Hot
450 - 475	230 - 240	8 - 9	Hottest

The Recipes That Aren't Here

We have not given recipes for the basic cooking of vegetables, as we assume most people know how to do this. However, we would like to stress the critical points of good vegetables, for taste and health:

1. Don't leave vegetables to soak for hours before cooking, or peel or chop them too early. Exposure to water causes nutrients to dissolve; exposure to air causes more vitamin break-down.

2. Use the minimum of water, or a steamer or pressure cooker basket, to reduce the contact with water. Keep cooking liquid for sauce and soup stock, unless you are cooking brassicas or potatoes, when it should be used within hours or not at all.

3. Bring the water to the boil, put vegetables in and cover tightly. This avoids the small amount of water evaporating. Reduce heat and simmer.

4. The smaller you chop vegetables, the quicker they will cook. But in general, take no notice of cookery book recommended times, which tend to be too long. Check most vegetables cut in slices or chunks after 4 minutes of cooking, then keep on checking at short intervals. Keep a record of times for future use. Your own garden produce will tend to cook quicker. If you add frozen vegetables to stews or soups, you need neither thaw nor cook them separately first. Add them only a few minutes before serving.

5. For speed, prepare vegetables in the order of longest required cooking time. This means, for instance, slicing potatoes or onions first and putting them on to cook, while you prepare carrots, swedes (rutabagas) or other root vegetables, finishing with the leafy greens and beanshoots.

Part 1
FAST, HEALTHY FOOD
Fast food — how it's done

The secrets of healthy meals in a hurry can be split into five basic steps:

1. CHOOSE the foods and recipes which happen to cook quickly — these include many of the healthiest dishes. Fish, which is lower in fat than meat, contains a more useful kind of fat and, in addition, is free from factory farming additives; it also happens to cook remarkably quickly.

    Being in a hurry is actually an advantage when it comes to making meals from fruit and vegetables: both taste their best and do you most good when least cooked, or when used fresh in salads. With the ideas given in this book, salads can become appealing and economical all the year round.

2. BALANCE the menu, using our five key guidelines of less fat, more fibre, less sugar, more fresh food, and less salt and additives. You're on the right track if you include at least one portion of fresh fruit and/or vegetables in every meal — from an orange with breakfast, to celery with cheese at tea-time. The only other element to think about is protein, although you don't need as much protein as people have long thought. A 3-4 oz (75-100g) helping of a protein-rich food is enough; nor does that automatically mean meat or fish, or even eggs or cheese. Grains such as wheat in bread, wholewheat pasta or pizza, or brown rice, millet and barley, all contain enough protein for a main course, especially as you'll find other bits of protein creeping into your meals without you realizing: milk in your drinks, a slice of wholemeal bread with soup, a little protein in potatoes or other vegetables — it all adds up. This book uses no meat, since the only quick-cooking meats are either the costly, child's-play chops and steaks or liver and other offal. The latter is very nutritious, but you can find plenty of recipes for them in ordinary cookbooks: this one is about foods you may never have thought of as 'convenience foods'. We do use fish in recipes, along with beans, seeds, nuts, cheese, yogurt and grains as protein foods. A 2 oz (50g) — raw weight — portion of wholewheat pasta, beans, lentils or brown rice is about right per person for a main course. With nuts and seeds, smaller amounts mixed with other proteins are better, since these foods provide so much oil along with their protein that you're liable to get too many calories *and* indigestion if

you use more than about 1 ½ oz (40g) per person as a portion as part of a recipe.

However, don't forget that not every meal has to be rich in protein: except for teenagers and those recovering from operations, most of us eat far more protein than we need. Lighter meals, based largely on fruit or vegetables, will improve your health, give your digestive system a rest, avoid weight problems and give you a general feeling of being nicely lean, rather than overfed after meals.

Don't forget that the protein part of a meal doesn't have to be in the main course. If you are a pudding fan, why not design meals around a salad or vegetable first course, followed by a pudding such as Instant Cheesecake (page 74), Little Egg Custards (page 110) or Gooseberry and Wheatgerm Dessert (page 80), supplying protein from soft cheese, eggs and milk, wheatgerm (25 per cent protein) and yogurt respectively.

Note: You will find more ideas for menu balancing in the next section.

3. TIME-AND-MOTION STUDY your recipe — a job we've mainly done for you in this book, so that you make up the recipe in the easiest, quickest sequence.

4. GET KITTED OUT with the equipment and the know-how which can save you time and effort. The ideas suggested on pages 17-20 can make all the difference between your coming up at the end of twenty minutes smiling, meal in hand, and feeling so tired after a somewhat longer 'cook-in' that you aren't even interested in eating.

5. STORE the natural foods that will help you prepare food quickly — and that doesn't mean rows of tins and mixes. See page 15 for some detailed suggestions, complete with reasons why, for instance, it's preferable to keep black-eye beans rather than black beans.

Seven More Tips for Speeding Things Up

1. Hundreds of savoury recipes start by asking you to *sauté* a sliced or chopped onion in fat for a few minutes, a process which brings out its flavour. Speed things up by:
    a. chopping your onion finely, so it softens quicker;
    b. cutting with a sharp knife in the method opposite, which gives a quick, fine-cut result.

1st cut
Halve onion vertically. Place flat side downwards on cutting board.

2nd cut
Holding onion together so it retains its shape, cut downwards making thin slices towards onion top.

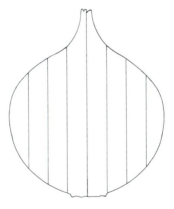

3rd cut
Holding onion firmly to avoid it slipping, make thin cuts across the previous slices.

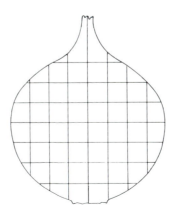

   c. You can also grate your onions (and other vegetables for faster cooking), on a coarse shredder. This method does, however, produce more tears, so if you are wearing make-up you want to keep, don't do it like this.

2.   Cook in batches, especially when it comes to grains and pulses. These don't suffer from a few days' keeping (refrigerated) after cooking, and for most recipes, you want to start with them cooked in any case.

    Cook enough red kidney beans for three meals, for instance, and you can use one third immediately in a salad; one third for a bean-and-vegetable curry; and the last batch for adding protein to a tomato-and-courgette mixture to pour over spaghetti or macaroni.

    A triple batch of brown rice gives you plain rice, to go with any savoury dish; the base for stuffed peppers or tomatoes; and either rice salad or a rice-and-vegetable hearty broth.

    A triple batch of chick peas (garbanzo beans) sets you up for a delicious pâté called *humus,* made by blending the cooked chick peas with garlic, tahini (sesame paste), a little olive oil and some soft cheese (see page 113 for exact details); then for a protein-packed soup made like the black-eye bean soup on page 66; and finally for a salad, mixed with cubes of cucumber, carrot and watercress, with cubes of red Cheshire cheese to complete a colourful main dish.

    Keep your stored grains and pulses covered in the refrigerator. You could freeze them, but the time taken for them to thaw out (and they don't recover their proper texture unless fully thawed) is longer than the cooking of a fresh batch.

3.   A white sauce (or in our case, the slightly creamier colour of a wholemeal sauce) occurs in several recipes. The quickest way of ensuring that this is smooth is to put the equal weights of fat and flour, and the milk or stock, in a liquidizer and whizz for a few seconds. Then heat, stirring slowly until it has thickened smoothly. If you still end up with lumps, reliquidize.

4.   When weighing out ingredients, it is often quicker to put the whole pack of what you are weighing from on the scales, see how much it weighs and then remove the required amount to bring the total down appropriately: eg. a half full pot of honey may weigh about 18 oz (550 g) including the jar. You want 2 oz (50 g), so you aim to remove enough to bring the total weight down to 1 lb (450 g)

    This method avoids constantly having to wash and dry the scale pan between messy items, such as honey, and means you only move the ingredients once — from pack to mixing bowl — not from pack to scale pan, and then to mixing bowl.

5. Beans and other pulses do have to be soaked before cooking — with the exceptions of split red lentils, split peas and black-eye beans. However, they *don't* have to be soaked overnight. Instead, you can start about an hour before you want to cook them, by washing thoroughly under the tap in a sieve, then bringing to the boil in plenty of water. When they boil, simmer for three minutes, turn heat off and leave beans to soak until you want them.

   Note: Little stones sometimes turn up in packets of beans, especially in chick peas (garbanzo beans). Look out for these when washing beans in sieve, and soaking. Use plenty of soaking water, and you improve the chances of any stones falling to the bottom of the pan. Then change the water carefully before cooking, so as not to mix the water (and maybe a stone or two) with the beans again.

6. Pastry-making does not come into most people's definition of quick cooking. It could, if every time you make pastry, you rub in twice the amount of fat and flour that you need at the time. Transfer the rest to a covered container in the refrigerator, and you need only mix it with water when you want it.

   This method is as fast as using a pastry mix, and thanks to the cold crumbs, produces better, shorter pastry. For tips on rolling out wholemeal pastry, see recipe for Flora Flan (page 68).

7. Use a pastry brush in a pot of vegetable oil to speed greasing dishes or tins, but also to help you use the minimum of fat. A quick brush round a frying pan gives you far less grease than a quick but haphazard pour of oil or lump of fat.

The Fast Larder

Rotate your stocks — aim to use up nuts, flour, grains, cereals and oils within three months, especially if you don't have a cool storage place.

Wholemeal flour: plain 100 per cent wholemeal or wholewheat (the same thing) is the most versatile. You can add different amounts of baking powder for different recipes, and also use it for bread. If you sometimes want lighter flour for baking, sieve your wholemeal and use the bran left in the sieve for another day — to add to cereal, casseroles or biscuits, for instance.

If you find working with one brand difficult, try another — and there is a fine-ground wholemeal which some people prefer for baking. However, for health purposes, the larger the particles of bran, the better.

Wholemeal pasta: spaghetti and macaroni lengths are the most useful, cooking in about 10-12 minutes. You can buy an organically grown brand from Italy (*Euvita*).

Brown rice: not part of the quick cook's repertoire unless you use either *Uncle Ben's* or *Whitworth's* brands, both of which cook in about 25 minutes, compared to the typical 40-50 minutes, because they are par-boiled.

Buckwheat: not really a grain, but a grass seed used like grain, a staple food in Russia. You can buy it unroasted or roasted (known by its Russian name of *kasha*). The roasted has much more flavour. You can roast your own, stirring gently in a dry, thick-based frying pan for a few minutes until it turns golden. This distinctive, pyramid-shaped grain has a special flavour, worth trying. Cooks in 15-20 minutes.

Millet: a small, yellow round grain you probably know from budgie sprays. Higher in protein than most grains, millet cooks in 15-20 minutes to a fluffy, pale cream colour. Its flavour is delicate — good for milk pudding lovers and those who condemn brown rice etc. as too dark and chewy.

Bulgur wheat: a par-boiled form of cracked wheat grain that is one of the most useful quick foods. As well as cooking to a small-grained, fluffy lightness in 15-20 minutes, it can be soaked for about the same time to make Tabbouleh, a tasty main-meal salad, see page 104.

Nuts: better bought whole, as they start to lose flavour and eventually become rancid once chopped or roasted. However, fresh, lightly toasted nuts have far more flavour than others. Turn them for a few minutes in a thick-based, ungreased frying pan over a low heat before grinding etc. Your choice will depend on your tastes, but here are some points to ponder: *hazelnuts* are substantially lower in fat and therefore in calories than other nuts, at 108 per ounce, compared with a typical 150 per ounce. *Walnuts* are one of the most complementary flavours for many sweet and savoury foods, and are also the nuts whose oil is highest in polyunsaturated essential fatty acids — about 150 calories per ounce. *Peanuts* have about 50 per cent more protein than other nuts — at 25 per cent protein, they match wheatgerm and outdo most meats. They are also very cheap. Against that, they are very high in oil too, with a calorie content of 170 calories per ounce. Highest in calories of all are *brazil nuts* (176), and *pecans* (about the same). Many people consider nuts too expensive for regular use. Remember that you only need about 1½ oz (40 g) per person per portion, which works out much cheaper than almost any meat.

Fats: on a well balanced diet, you won't use too many added fats. However, you still want to get maximum food value out of the ones you do use. For cooking, two kinds of oil will do most jobs, with *cold-pressed olive oil* the best for Mediterranean recipes and for high temperatures. For essential fatty acids, however, use either *safflower, sunflower* or *soya oil,* all for salads. Soya oil has a distinctive taste — try before you buy a lot of it.

For spreading, you don't have to give up *butter.* Just use less of it, or mix it with *polyunsaturated margarine.* There is no point nutritionally in buying any margarine that does not say on the label 'high in polyunsaturates'. Although other vegetable margarines will contain barely any cholesterol, they have generally had a substantial part of their fats artificially hardened, changing unsaturated fats into saturated ones like animal fats. Only very soft fats — mainly oils and that includes fish oils — provide the essential fatty acids. If you use *low-fat spreads,* you are getting a reasonable level of polyunsaturates, where the essential fatty acids are found.

Fats very high in polyunsaturates do not tolerate high heats well.

Sweeteners: as you will be using little sugar on a real food regime, the lightest-tinted of the raw cane sugars, *Demerara,* is probably your best bet if you only want to buy one kind. It contains fewer minerals than the darker sugars, treacle or molasses, but is the most versatile. You can use it for the electrician's tea with the minimum of complaints, for marmalade and for delicate-flavoured dishes without drowning them in treacle flavour. Make sure whatever brown sugar you buy is 'raw' cane sugar, not 'restored' white beet. The key is the label: it should show the country of origin as being somewhere exotic, such as Guyana, Malawi, Demerara itself or somewhere in the West Indies.

Honey is slightly preferable to sugar: it provides a slightly sweeter (so use less) taste per ounce for slightly fewer calories — about 85 compared to sugar's 110. It is also mainly a kind of sugar the body usually needs less insulin to digest. You can use honey in place of sugar in most recipes except biscuits, jams and cakes, where special recipes are needed.

Molasses is like a more intense kind of treacle, to be used sparingly. It's got more nutrients and only about two-thirds as many calories as even brown sugar, and adds special flavour to cakes like gingerbread, chutneys, and some sweet-sour type savouries.

Pulses: the only ones suitable for the quick cook are *split red lentils,* and *black-eye beans.* Both need no soaking and cook quickly — 15-20 minutes for lentils, 35 minutes for the beans. If you can cook ahead for meals in a hurry, next choices would be chick peas (garbanzo beans), butter beans (Lima beans) and red kidney beans — three varieties of the many available that are versatile and popular. You may also consider keeping a tin or two of *cooked beans* on hand for emergencies — even some of those in tomato sauce, which despite their sugar content are one of the best convenience tins.

Seeds: useful garnishes and flavourings, *sunflower, sesame, poppy and pumpkin seeds* are all best when lightly toasted; see nuts section for method. Remember that they also add protein and essential fatty acids to a wide range of dishes, such as biscuits, muesli, fruit salad, risotto, breads and flans. If you are a calorie-counter, reckon on an average 160 calories per ounce.

Sesame seeds must be crushed for their full flavour to come out — as well as helping their general digestion. They are rich in calcium, but you won't get much of it unless they are ground, best done after toasting lightly. Pumpkin seeds might well be labelled 'the seeds for men'! They are a specific herbal remedy for prostate trouble, at the rate of about 30 seeds a day (in conjunction with diet and exercise treatment).

Dried fruit: so useful to eat plain or in many recipes needing little time to make; keep dried *apricots, block dates, sultanas (golden seedless raisins)* or *raisins* and *Hunza apricots* on hand. The kind of apricots that claim 'no need to soak' are no great advantage, and much more expensive. You don't really need to soak apricots anyway. The easiest way to wash dried fruit, whose countries of origin, except the U.S.A., are not generally noted for hygiene, is to boil it for a minute or two, then throw away the water and start from scratch. This also helps remove sulphur dioxide from pale fruit like apricots, sultanas, apple rings, peaches, pears and nectarines. The sulphur is used to preserve them and their pale tint. Avoid buying fruit which has had mineral oil (liquid paraffin) applied to it: it's not healthy stuff.

Food in tins: worth keeping for speed and chosen for lack of additives (except for salt) are: *tinned tomatoes* and *tomato purée (paste)* (buy the latter in jars if possible to avoid reaction with metal lining of tubes and tins); *sardines, tuna fish* and other *fish,* which do not lose food value in canning, and which provide useful sources of vitamins A and D, essential fatty acids and quick meals. For fewer non-useful fats and calories, look for those tinned in sauce or brine, rather than oil; *sweetcorn* (also available frozen); *fruit tinned in natural juice; all-fruit jams* in jars (such as *Whole Earth* varieties); *a few tins of 'nutmeat',* mixtures of nuts, grain and seasoning, to be eaten hot or cold, are useful emergency stores.

Flavourings: yeast extract and *soya/tamari sauce* are extremely useful; *cloves, ground cinnamon, mixed spice, ginger, curry powder; sea salt, 'vegetized salt'* (with vegetable extracts, giving more flavour for less salt) or *potassium-based salt substitute* (*Ruthmol* etc.); *nutmeg, black* and *white peppercorns* provide a much better flavour when you grind them as you want them; some form of *stock powder* or cube that is additive-free — health food stores sell a selection; herbs to include *thyme, bay leaves, mixed dried herbs, oregano, ground cumin, basil, tarragon, garlic and sweet cicely; vanilla pods,* or for speed, *natural vanilla essence; almond essence; Worcestershire sauce; tahini* — sesame paste; *HP sauce* (yes, it's all natural).

Miscellaneous: gelatine or agar agar (a seaweed extract with strong gelling properties, for vegetarians). *cornflour* (cornstarch) — you can use maize flour (cornmeal) from health food stores, but as you use so little of this item, its refined nature won't matter much; vinegar — *cider vinegar* is preferred for its high potassium and other mineral content.

The stores you make: when you have cooking time, lay up useful extras for quick meals. Some — like *ratafias, mincemeat, apricot spread* and *rollmops* — are detailed in the sections in Thinking Ahead and Useful Extras. Also useful are *chutney, lemon curd* (which you can make with honey), *wholemeal breadcrumbs* (bake bread in slow oven until very dry, then crumble with rolling pin in polythene bag).

Refrigerator stores: fruit and vegetables keep better in the bottom of a refrigerator, making them easier to keep on hand.

If you use a freezer, *wholemeal bread* freezes well for at least three months. Freeze it sliced — then you can defrost a slice instantly in the toaster, instead of waiting for the whole loaf to thaw. *Fish* and *fish cakes* (recipe on page 55) can be cooked or reheated without thawing, provided the fishcakes don't include rice. Home-grown, pick-your-own or other *soft fruit* (except strawberries, which freeze poorly) is a good freezer stand-by, together with *vegetables* for emergency use when you don't have fresh.

Although many of the dishes in this book freeze well, the time they take to thaw means that they aren't so useful as quick meals unless you think ahead — when you could cook from scratch anyway.

Worthwhile Investments
If you regularly cook in a hurry — or just like to spend as little time as possible on food preparation — buying the right equipment will actually save you money. That's because if you don't have the aids to quick cooking, you'll find yourself spending more on ready-made or take-away foods when you can't face an hour in the kitchen. Having the tools would make the job far less off-putting — they really do save you time — and the meal you make at home is likely to be considerably healthier too.

We suggest that the following items are investments worth considering. You won't want them all — they're the range from which to choose:

★ *A liquidizer or blender* not only speeds up many recipes, but saves food value too. It means, for instance, that you can make *purées* (sauces) to thicken soups or puddings, rather than doing the job with cream, butter or eggs. And while you *can purée* by laborious sieving, that requires that the vegetables or fruit be cooked to a much softer state — longer cooking which will have reduced their vitamin content. If you buy the type of blender that fits on top of a small coffee grinder, you will also have the means to make breadcrumbs and grind nuts neatly and quickly.

We consider a liquidizer such an essential to fast meals that we have assumed that one is available in many of the recipes. They are not very expensive — and if you don't want to get one, please make sure that you do acquire a really strong sieve.

★ *A set of good knives* will speed up every recipe, while actually reducing your chances of cutting yourself. Most cuts start with a blunt knife slipping on the surface of food, when a sharp one would have gone safely through to the board beneath. We recommend *Victorinox* stainless steel knives, which do not need sharpening and won't darken the fruit and vegetables they cut, as ordinary steel knives may do.

A peeler is useful: although it's better to retain the food value in fruit and vegetable skins, you will sometimes want to peel them to get rid of blemishes or doubtful chemical residues. Some foods demand them: kiwi fruit, for instance are hard to peel even with a sharp knife. A peeler eases these jobs and also reduces the thickness of the skin you remove, minimizing nutrient loss and food wastage.

★ *A strong, square-based grater,* made of stainless steel, will make vegetable shredding an easy job. The square shape gives you a firm non-slip base to press down on safely, as well as a choice of shredding blades. These graters are also easy to clean: it's worth having one for small jobs even if you also have a more sophisticated chopper.

If you do a lot of vegetable or fruit processing, however, a *Mouli Legume* — a hand-operated shredder with a variety of discs for shreds and slices — is an excellent economical item. Easy to wash, they produce attractively even-cut results, quickly.

★ *A nut grater* is useful if you don't have a coffee mill or *Mouli Legume,* both of which will do this job. The *Mouli Junior* is a reasonable hand grinder for smallish amounts of nuts. The next one up in the *Mouli* range is the same size, but with three drums, so you can shred finely or coarsely, or slice nuts, vegetables or fruit.

★ *A food processor or Kenwood Chef* will do all the jobs of the liquidizer, nut grater and square grater — as well as those of a beater, mincer, and often a lot more. Their appeal depends partly on whether you already have some items of kitchen equipment which they would duplicate. But it is also very much a question of your personal style. They are bulky items, and unless you keep yours on the worktop, ready to use, you will probably find you are deterred from making full use of it by the chore of getting it out of a cupboard and storing it away again. Some snazzy kitchen units incorporate a lift-up platform specially designed to keep such machines out of sight yet ready in seconds.

These machines will also do the work of a mixer, mincer and egg white whisker. The *Kenwood Chef* does the last job notably more efficiently than most food processors. In general, the *Kenwood* has a bigger capacity than food processors, so it will take a larger quantity of cake mix or dough. When it comes to making yeast doughs, the *Kenwood's* dough hook makes it much more powerful than the food processors. The *Kenwood* also has some unique attachments, such as a pasta maker, a wheat mill for home-produced fresh flour, a cream maker and more. The only points against it are that you have to pay extra for most attachments, and that you need somewhere to store them.

Food processors are a little more limited, both in capacity (although they work so quickly that splitting food into batches does not make processing that much lengthier) and functions. They don't beat air into cake mixtures or egg whites so efficiently as either the *Kenwood Chef* or other mixers (or you, with a strong arm, could). If you do buy one, and you are interested in making juice, check that the brand you choose has this optional extra available.

On the plus side, food processors are generally neater and take less space. They do more of their tasks with the basic goblet and blades, so need fewer attachments or space to store them.

★ *An egg whisk* Healthy cookery uses a good deal of whisked egg whites to give lightness to more fibrous ingredients. If you have a cake mixer, that will do the job for you, but otherwise a little 'balloon' whisk or larger hand egg whisk is needed. These are surprisingly efficient, ideally used in a narrow vessel like a jug. Whisking egg whites with a fork is only recommended for strengthening the wrists.

★ *Fancy cutters, ramekins and ring moulds* may sound highly unnecessary luxuries. In our view, they have a practical purpose. This is to give the quickest meal a sense of form and pattern which positively adds to its eye appeal. Shapes make meals look more professional too, which is often helpful if you are serving up something less familiar. It gives the eaters confidence that this is a tried and tested dish, even if it is new to them.

Here are some of the most useful items: *biscuit cutters* with a variety of shapes, such as a gingerbread man or woman, animals or a Christmas tree shape; *individual casseroles,* each holding about ½ pint (300 ml or 1 ¼ cups), which have the dual benefit of shortening the cooking times of dishes such as *soufflés* or custard, as well as making them look especially appealing — everyone likes having their own little dish; *a white, fluted-edge flan dish,* oven-proof, which makes many savoury and sweet dishes look more attractive on the table; *patty tins,* since buns cook much quicker than loaves, and small quiches faster than large ones. You also can use roomy patty tins for making muffins, mince pies, popovers and mini-Yorkshire puddings.

★ A *wide-mouthed vacuum flask* enables you to keep casseroles hot instead of reheating them; to widen the range of packed meals to include hot dishes that would be difficult to extract from a narrow-mouthed flask; to put on a flaskful of dried fruit at the start of a meal, and have hot *compote* ready by pudding time; to make porridge without stirring or sticky washing up; and to make home-made yogurt between times. Make sure it is a *vacuum* and not an *insulation* flask. The latter retains heat with a layer of foam, which has the advantage over the vacuum flask's metal liner of being unbreakable. However, it loses heat more quickly, so it is not so successful for cooking in.

    Flasks retain heat longer when they are full, so don't buy a very large model if you usually cook in small amounts. You can also use a flask for finishing cooking some dishes started on the stove. Boil soaked beans on the stove for 10 to 15 minutes, for instance, and you can finish the cooking by tipping them into a heated flask for about an hour. This is useful if you want to forget cooking while you do something else, and also saves fuel.

★ A *pressure cooker* is an obvious aid to speedy cooking. We usually suggest using stainless steel models, to avoid any possible interaction between food and aluminium, or any allergy to aluminium.

    Depending on the pressure of your cooker, cooking times will be divided by two or three. Because pressure cooking shortens cooking times, it can improve the retention of vitamins and minerals. On the other hand, it becomes much easier to overcook vegetables and fruit. So consult the instruction booklet for times, and then set a timer .

★ A *timer* is also useful when you are in a hurry, because you are likely to be doing more than one job at once. While you are concentrating on one, you may allow another to burn or dry up.

    Use your timer when baking with wholemeal flour: because it is naturally brown, you can't see by the browning colour when pastry or biscuits are cooked. If you wait for a colour change, the dish may be overbaked.

★ A *cast-iron skillet pan* will save you time in washing up — they conduct heat well and rarely stick; aggravation — they cook food evenly, avoiding burnt spots; and calories — they need less fat than easier-sticking pans.

Healthy food — how it's done

Confused about what healthy eating really means? Take these five guidelines to heart, and you're set to choose the healthiest meals wherever you are:

1. *Choose leaner foods* Eating too much fat is the outstanding fault in the British diet — because excess fat is firmly linked with excess calories. Fat has 9 calories per gram, or 255 per ounce when pure as in oil or lard. That's more than twice as many calories as protein (4 calories per gram) or carbodydrate (3.75 per gram). The average person eats 50 per cent more fat than is good for his health.

As well as encouraging overweight, excess fat, especially hard fat, is linked with the rise in levels of fat, cholesterol and pressure in the arteries associated with high risks of heart disease, strokes and other circulation problems. Don't try to cut fat out, but do cut it down, not just by avoiding frying and heavy spreads of butter or margarine, but also by dodging hidden fats — in cream, hard cheese, nuts, red meat, pastry, chocolate, biscuits, cakes and salad dressings, for instance. A little of these from time to time is fine; but use them daily and you're building trouble for yourself.

Healthy cookery leans more towards the lower fat foods: wholemeal bread, cereals and other grains, beans and lentils, low-fat cheeses and skimmed or semi-skimmed milk, plain yogurt, egg whites rather than yolks, fish and chicken instead of red meat, and lots of fruit and vegetables.

2. *Choose more fibre* Roughage or fibre is the part of carbohydrates in grains, beans, fruit, vegetables and nuts that is not digested but travels through us, 'padding' other wastes and helping efficient and speedy elimination. Fibre 'dilutes' food, and the importance of this effect is still being investigated. For practical purposes, however, you don't have to wait for science: eating more fibre, as people have always done until this century, is both a prudent and a digestion-aiding policy. You don't have to eat bran, however. The recipes in this book are almost all fairly high in fibre anyway. When you eat wholemeal bread and cereals, plenty of fresh vegetables and fruit, and make more use of beans, grains, seeds and nuts, you don't need extra bran.

3. *Choose less sugar*   Wherever possible, our recipes whittle down the amount of sugar necessary, or avoid it completely. Sugar is very high in calories, especially when you realize that you don't get anything except calories from it — barely one of the vitamins, minerals, protein substances or kinds of fibre we need to maintain health. As sugar is also very 'more-ish', it is easy to let it take up so many of our calories per day (110 per ounce, white or brown) that we reduce our chances of getting all the nutrients we really need.

Raw cane sugar is used in our recipes because it does at least contain a few trace elements, such as chromium, which the body uses to digest sugar. But you don't need *any* sugar — it does not give any magical kind of energy. Doubt that? Remember that it was never used in Europe until a few hundred years ago; and remember that sugar rots your teeth!

4.   *Choose more fresh foods*   Fruit and vegetables provide many of the vitamins, minerals and roughage that help protect our health, and they have a low score in terms of calories. They also offer variety, colour and flavour in meals to divert our attention away from rich, greasy food.

5. *Avoid added salt*   Eating too much salt tends to encourage high blood pressure in vulnerable people, and having high blood pressure is a clear sign that you are much more likely to suffer a heart attack, stroke or kidney problems. Cutting down sharply on added salt has been shown to help reduce high blood pressure remarkably quickly. The substance in salt which can affect one's health is sodium, and this is balanced in the body by another element, potassium. Drugs to control high blood pressure make the body lose the potassium it needs (as well as having other side-effects). Although too much salt is not usually the only factor causing high blood pressure (it is also worsened by smoking, overweight and lack of exercise), controlling its use in the diet is one of the easiest preventive measures. At the same time, eat more potassium, naturally found in fruit and vegetables. Cutting down on sodium means cutting down on processed foods, which almost all have added salt. By doing so, you will also be cutting down on the fat and sugar which these foods tend to be rich in, as well as limiting your intake of food additives.

Choosing Balanced Menus
The principles of balancing menus can be done with a saying, rather like the one for brides of 'something old, something new, something borrowed, something blue'.

For meals, it would run something like this: 'Something fresh, something bright, protein next, but keep it light'. Here are some examples:

1. *10 minutes*

Chinese Vegetables — provide the greenery and if you include carrots, peppers, peas or swedes (rutabagas), this will also look colourful and bright.

Instant Cheesecake — provides the protein for the meal, without you eating a lot of fat with it, thanks to using low-fat cheese. This menu also provides a good texture contrast: a hot crunchy main course, and a cool, smooth dessert.

2. *20 minutes*

Fish pie — provides protein not only from the fish, but from the peas or beans in the recipe, and a little from the milk in the binding sauce as well as the potato topping.

Oat and Honey Grapefruit — a fresh, citrus taste with a completely different texture. Reasonable colour contrast in this menu, providing you don't overcook the vegetables for the pie; best if you use smoked fish — not the dyed sort — (for yellow) and pink grapefruit.

3. *30 minutes*

California Platter — a colourful fruit platter, with cottage cheese and nuts providing some protein.

Rhubarb Crumble — a relatively solid dessert, with some protein coming from wholewheat flour in the topping. A cold, crisp first course with a hot, comforting pudding.

4. *10 minutes*

Grilled Fish, with green vegetables or mushrooms — the protein in your meal, but not carrying much fat with it. The fresh and bright part comes from the vegetables.

Raisin and Apple Scotch Pancakes — for a more satisfying meal, with more protein from wheat, egg and milk in the pancakes, and also fibre from flour, raisins and apples.

or

Stewed Rhubarb — which complements fish in flavour, and is a pretty colour. Use the recipe for Rhubarb Crumble (page 84), omitting topping.

5. *20 minutes*

Vulgar Bulgur — protein from wheat and hazelnuts. A fairly dry, risotto-like texture dish, which includes vegetables for your 'fresh' part.

Grilled Bananas — a moister texture, interesting-looking (no complaints that healthy foods are all dull-looking), with slightly unusual colour and shape.

6. *30 minutes*

Lentil Soup — hearty, smooth, golden-coloured soup which provides a good contribution of protein, especially if eaten with wholemeal rolls.

Salad - a big mixed selection of shredded vegetables, including something green, and with a little cheese or nuts if liked. — your fresh, colourful element, with protein from any cheese, nuts, or cooked grain used, more if you use a yogurt dressing.

Part 2
RECIPES
Ten Minute Main Courses

Peanut patties

A basic recipe that can be varied, using other nuts and herbs, to make a variety of tasty, quick main course savouries.

(Serves 4 — about 310 calories each.)

Imperial (Metric)

2 oz (50g) finely chopped or grated onion
2 oz (50g) chopped mushrooms
1 tablespoonful vegetable oil
2 oz (50g) ground peanuts
2 oz (50g) ground sunflower seeds
2 oz (50g) grated cheese
2 tablespoonsful lemon juice
1 tablespoonful soya sauce
1 tablespoonful chopped parsley
Tahini (sesame paste) to bind
Wholemeal breadcrumbs or
    wheatgerm to coat

American

½ cupful finely chopped or grated onion
1 cupful chopped mushrooms
1 tablespoonful + 1 teaspoonful vegetable oil
½ cupful ground peanuts
½ cupful ground sunflower seeds
½ cupful grated cheese
2 tablespoonsful + 2 teaspoonsful lemon juice
1 tablespoonful + 1 teaspoonful soya sauce
1 heaping tablespoonful chopped parsley
Tahini (sesame paste) to bind
Wholemeal breadcrumbs or
    wheatgerm to coat

Turn onion and mushrooms in about quarter of the oil for a few minutes. Meanwhile, mix all other ingredients except tahini and breadcrumbs/ wheatgerm, adding onion and mushrooms after softening. Add enough tahini to make mixture stick together without being too tacky. Divide into four patties, coat with breadcrumbs or wheatgerm and *sauté* in remaining oil or grill for a few minutes on each side.

Smoked mackerel pâté ✓

This rich-flavoured, smooth-textured pâté can transform a variety of plain foods into satisfying main dishes. Pile it next to a mixed salad; or on to a mashed potato; into a pitta bread with green salad; heat gently to top a plate of lightly cooked courgettes (zucchini), carrots, cauliflower, or broccoli; generously heap it on to an open sandwich, with watercress; serve as a hot topping for pasta; as a flan filling, diluted in richness with 2 cupsful of lightly cooked courgettes (zucchini) or peas.

(Serves 4 — about 220 calories each.)

Imperial (Metric)	American
12 oz (275g) smoked mackerel or kipper	1 ½ cupsful smoked mackerel or kipper
or 2 tins of sardines, drained of oil	*or* 2 tins of sardines, drained of oil
4 oz (100g) low-fat soft cheese	½ cupful low-fat soft cheese
Juice of a lemon	Juice of a lemon
Handful of parsley	Handful of parsley
2 tablespoonsful natural yogurt, thick	2 heaped tablespoonsful natural yogurt, thick

If using kipper, poach for 2 minutes in jug of boiling water. Remove skin and any bones from fish unless using sardines. Mash with a fork, then mix in the soft cheese (sieve, if using cottage cheese). Add lemon juice and most of parsley, chopped in with scissors. Now add yogurt, withholding some if texture of pâté, which should be thick, becomes too soft.

No-smell kippers ✓

When you think of kippers, does the idea of a lingering aroma in the kitchen put you off? This way is virtually smell-free and there's no spattered grill or frying pan (skillet) to scrub either. Kippers are one of the richest sources of vitamin D, so if you are not vegetarian, build them into your shopping list once a week, especially in winter when vitamin D from sunshine is hard to find. Choose Manx kippers whenever you can: they are free from added colour. Frozen kippers can be cooked straight from the freezer, but take a few minutes longer.

(Serves 4 — about 220 calories each for a typical 7 oz kipper.)

1 kipper or 1-2 fillets per person

Boil a large kettle of water (or a large frying pan/skillet of water, if using still frozen kippers). Place kippers in heat-proof, shallow dish or tail-upwards in deep jug. Cover with boiling water and then with a lid or plate. Leave for 4 minutes before removing with egg slice to serve with brown toast and greens. If using frozen fish, immerse in frying pan (skillet) and simmer gently for about 8 minutes, covered.

Note: You can use the same method to poach finnan haddie.

Spanish omelette

Everyone knows about omelettes, scrambled eggs and boiled eggs as quick meals. Here's a variation that's less 'eggy' and easy to prepare for several people.

(Serves 4 — about 210 calories each, but about 100 higher if using cheese or nut toppings.)

Imperial (Metric)	American
1 large onion, sliced thinly	1 large onion, sliced thinly
2 boiled potatoes, or 1 cupful cooked brown rice or wholemeal pasta	2 boiled potatoes or 1 ¼ cupsful cooked brown rice or wholemeal pasta
1 tablespoonful vegetable oil	1 tablespoonful + 1 teaspoonful vegetable oil
2 (140g) tomatoes or small tin	1 cupful tomatoes or small tin
4 eggs	4 eggs

Plus 1 cupful/1 ¼ cupsful each of at least 2 of these: cooked vegetables, cooked fish, cubed cheese, whole or chopped nuts, sliced mushrooms.

Using a thick-based frying pan (skillet), ideally cast iron, fry onions, potatoes (or rice or pasta), and mushrooms (if using) in half the fat for 4 minutes. Add tomatoes and any other flavouring you're using. Cook for 2 minutes longer. Meanwhile, beat the eggs and season well.

   Stir contents of pan to ensure that nothing is sticking. Then move to one side while you use remaining fat to re-oil pan. Now spread contents of pan evenly, pour eggs over, stir over low-to-medium heat until underneath is just set. Heat grill, brown top slightly under it. Loosen with a slice and cut into portions as if it were a flan.

Cheese and oat burgers

This looks as if it doesn't make enough for four, but it's very filling.

(Serves 4 — about 190 calories each.)

Imperial (Metric)
3 oz (75g) sharp Cheddar cheese
2 oz (50g) rolled oats
1 egg
1 teaspoonful mixed herbs
1 tablespoonful sesame seeds
   (optional)
Freshly ground black pepper
A few wholemeal breadcrumbs for
   coating

American
1 cupful (scant) sharp Cheddar
   cheese
1 cupful rolled oats
1 egg
1 teaspoonful mixed herbs
¼ cupful sesame seeds (optional)
Freshly ground black pepper
A few wholemeal breadcrumbs for
   coating

Heat grill and lightly oil grill pan. If using sesame seeds, toast in dry frying pan (skillet) over a low heat for a minute or two, then crush slightly with end of rolling pin. Grate cheese and mix with oats, egg, herbs and seeds if using. Season with pepper.

Shape into four patties, dip in crumbs and grill for a few minutes on each side.

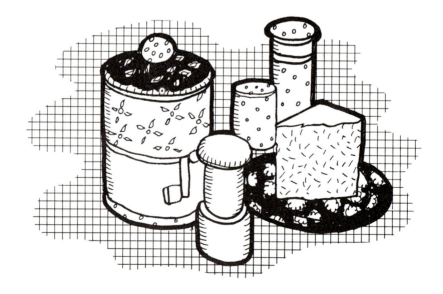

Chinese vegetables

One of the best fast meals — both for the result, and from a nutritional viewpoint.

(Serves 4 — about 175 calories each.)

Imperial (Metric)	**American**
About 2 lb (900g) mixed fresh vegetables — e.g. 1 onion, 1 large carrot, ¼ small cabbage, 1 parsnip, 1 stick celery, handful of mushrooms, handful of green beans, 3 oz (75g) peas	About 2 pounds mixed fresh vegetables — e.g. 1 onion, 1 large carrot, ¼ small cabbage, 1 parsnip, 1 stick celery, handful of mushrooms, handful of green beans, ½ cupful peas
1 tablespoonful vegetable oil	1½ tablespoonsful vegetable oil
2 teaspoonsful soya/tamari sauce	2 teaspoonsful soya/tamari sauce
¼ pint (150ml) water	1¼ cupsful water
2 teaspoonsful cornflour	2 teaspoonsful cornstarch
2 oz (50g) cashew nuts or almonds or hazelnuts	⅓ cupful cashew nuts or almonds or hazelnuts
Good pinch of Demerara sugar	Good pinch of Demerara sugar
2 teaspoonsful sweet sherry	2 teaspoonsful sweet sherry

Peel and chop onion finely. Heat large frying pan/skillet (or wok) brushed with the oil. *Sauté* onion while you wash and chop other vegetables fairly thinly, working in order of hardness, so that carrot or swede (rutabaga) would be cut first and added as prepared to onion. When all vegetables are added (withold peas or beansprouts until later if using), turn vegetables constantly over fairly high heat for about 4 minutes. Mix cornflour (cornstarch), sherry, sugar, soya sauce and water, add to pan with nuts, stir in and cover pan for 2 minutes. Remove lid, stir again for a few minutes more, only until vegetables are cooked but still crispy. If using peas or beansprouts, add now, heating for about 1 minute. Serve with more soya/tamari sauce.

Tjatjiki

A Greek appetizer, to serve as a first course or as part of a main course. Stuffed into wholemeal pitta bread, with hard-boiled egg sliced in too, this makes a delicious and simple main dish.

(Serves 4 — about 48 calories each.)

Imperial (Metric)	American
1 cucumber (about 1 lb/450g)	1 cucumber (about 1 pound)
8 fl oz (300ml) natural yogurt, thick	1 cupful natural yogurt, thick
1 clove of crushed garlic (optional)	1 clove of crushed garlic (optional)
Juice of 1 lemon	Juice of 1 lemon
Chives or parsley	Chives or parsley
A pinch of sea salt and black	A pinch of sea salt and black
pepper	pepper

Chop the cucumber finely or grate it coarsely. Stir in yogurt, crushed garlic, lemon juice, chopped chives or parsley and season to taste. Serve sprinkled with more chives or parsley.

Variation: you can exchange the cucumber for green pepper and chopped tomatoes.

Grilled fish ✓

One of the most neglected 'convenience foods', fish makes the quickest, tastiest, simplest meals. Almost any fish is suitable, whole or in fillets or steaks. Unless they are very thick, fillets can be grilled without turning, while whole fish and thick steaks only need turning once.

You don't have a handy fishmonger? While fresh fish is worth hunting for, frozen fish can be cooked straight from the freezer unless you are using a large, whole fish.

(Serves 4 — white fish about 25 calories per ounce; trout about 38 per ounce; herrings, mackerel, salmon about 60-65 calories per ounce, all for raw weights. Oily fish like herrings lose calories when grilled, as fat melts out.)

1-1 ½ lb (450-675g) fish

Heat grill well, and grease grill pan. For minimum washing up, line with foil and grease that. Grill fish for about 2-3 minutes on each side, testing for tenderness with a fork. Avoid overcooking, when fish will quickly become dry and unappetizing. For an all-in-one meal, grill mushrooms and tomatoes alongside the fish.

Variations: if you don't grease fish at all, it will develop a crisp surface, which has some of the appeal of barbecued food, and a charred flavour which is good provided the inside of the fish is still moist. Add more flavours by sprinkling the fish with your choice of ★ sesame seeds ★ soya/tamari sauce ★ lemon juice ★ finely sliced onions ★ chopped fennel (delicate aniseed flavour) ★ slivers of almond ★ a few drops of Worcestershire sauce and 1 teaspoonful curry powder mixed with 1 teaspoonful margarine to hold it on to the fish ★ paper-thin slices of root ginger ★ coarsely ground black pepper and rolled oats or fine oatmeal ★ paprika ★ mild German or French mustard ★ tomato *purée* (paste) with a little margarine, spread on.

You can help these flavourings stick to the fish by brushing it with a little oil or lemon juice. Alternative 'glues' are peanut butter, tahini/sesame paste and your favourite chutneys.

If using small whole fish, such as trout, flavour from the inside too, with sprigs of herbs such as fennel or lemon thyme, or chopped mushrooms.

Sandwiches

Nobody needs recipes for sandwiches. So this is more a reminder that sandwiches are quite high enough in protein and other nutrients to make a main meal.

Avoid choosing high-fat fillings like peanut butter or cream cheese very often. 'Think lean' with salad fillings; mashed banana, lean chicken, mashed fish, cottage cheese and all the permutations possible between cottage cheese and flavourings like cucumber, mashed salmon, chives or chutney.

Naturally, you're better off with wholemeal bread (61 calories per ounce — less than white). Spread it meanly with butter or soft vegetable margarine; or more generously with a mixture between these and cottage cheese; with cottage or medium-fat curd cheese alone; or with low-fat spread.

Many people who find it impossible to see a sandwich as a meal can more easily accept open Danish-style sandwiches, or toasted sandwiches as a 'real' meal. Sandwich toasters come complete with lots of suggestions for interesting fillings. Particularly attractive for speed and flavour are: fresh green herbs, washed, chopped and spread with cottage cheese; grated carrot mixed half-and-half with grated cheese; pizza-style fillings, with tomatoes, olives, mushrooms, cheese and oregano; 1 tablespoonful each peanut butter and chopped celery, mixed with 2 tablespoonsful grated cheese and sprinkled with a few chopped walnuts (English walnuts); or bread soaked in egg, flavoured with honey, raisins and cinnamon, with slices of apple in between, then toasted.

Soup

With the addition of soup, many light but well balanced meals which we would otherwise regard as mere snacks become complete 'proper' meals. Soup completes a sandwich or salad meal, especially in cold weather when, psychologically, we want something hot to eat.

The quickest soups are naturally made from the quickest-cooking vegetables — mushrooms, courgettes (zucchini), spinach and watercress are ideal. A liquidizer or blender is the other ingredient that makes quick soups both possible and easy. Finally, a pressure cooker puts any soup recipe that would normally take up to 30 minutes in the 10-minute category.

But let's look at non-pressure cooker quick soups. As with most soup recipes, the key to good flavour is stock. If you keep a stock jug in the refrigerator as a matter of course, adding any vegetable or meat cooking water as you get it, soup and sauce stock will always be handy. Don't add the water from cooking potatoes or any kind of brassica (cabbage, cauliflower, sprouts or broccoli) — they will not keep.

If you use a covered jug with measures on the side for stock, you will find it easier both to register when it's time to use your stock for soup or sauce (or to cook rice, risotto or beans in), and to measure it out. Don't keep stock more than a few days, even in the fridge. When you use stock, you get the benefit of vitamins and minerals which are dissolved into it from the vegetables, grains or other food cooked in it. You also avoid the additives of bought stock cubes, and possibly unwanted extra calories and fat from using milk stock.

However, those extra calories are sometimes what you want to make a more substantial soup. Even if you don't have a stock jug, you can avoid the distinctive monosodium glutamate flavours of most bought cubes. Health food stores sell a variety of additive-free stock cubes and flavouring granules. Yeast extract or soya/tamari sauce are almost indispensable for the soup maker. Tomato *purée* (paste) and tinned tomatoes or tomato juice are also very useful. Then there are herbs, which are important to the variety as well as quality of soup flavours. Bay leaves, tarragon and parsley are especially useful. Bay leaves seem to add depth to the flavour of soup. Tarragon adds a fresh, lemony tang which enhances many soups. Parsley should be used in far larger quantities than recipes suggest — it's only then that you enjoy its flavour properly. If your recipe ends by putting the soup through a blender, this will be the time to add most herbs (not bay leaf) or parsley, without chopping problems — just scissor-cut a handful into the blender goblet. Don't let herbs cook for long.

The following recipes can be varied by using different vegetables, once you have the basic method. Recipes increasingly prefer to thicken soups with a *purée* (paste), rather than with flour, cream or eggs, the traditional methods. The advantage in calorie terms can be considerable, as well as making the preparation simpler. Most soups also taste good when chilled, and served with some natural yogurt mixed in.

Making More of Soup

To make soups more of a meal, and also grander in appearance: ★ add cooked rice, cooked beans or cooked pasta to the finished soup; ★ sprinkle toasted flaked almonds on top of a creamy-thick soup; ★ to make wholewheat Melba toast, cut thick slices of bread and toast on both sides. Heat grill. Lay bread flat on board, and carefully cut through horizontally to make 2 thin slices. Toast untoasted side carefully, allowing room for bread to curl without hitting grill and singeing.

Store in air-tight tin, recrisping if necessary with a few minutes on a baking tray in the oven before serving. ★ Spread bread sparingly with margarine or butter and *Marmite*, then grill on both sides, cut into quarters and serve with soup.

Watercress soup

(Serves 4 — about 186 calories each, or 139 using either half water or all skim milk.)

Imperial (Metric)	American
1 onion	1 onion
1 carrot	1 carrot
1 oz (25g) butter or soft vegetable margarine	¼ cupful butter or soft vegetable margarine
1 oz (25g) wholemeal plain flour	¼ cupful wholemeal plain flour
1 pint (600ml) milk *or* ½ milk: ½ water	2 ½ cupsful milk or mixture of milk and water
1 bunch watercress	2 cupsful watercress
Juice of half a lemon	Juice of half a lemon
Sea salt and black pepper	Sea salt and black pepper

Peel onion and carrot, grate both into pan lightly greased with the fat. *Sauté* gently for a few minutes, add flour. Stir in over low heat. Remove from heat, and gradually work in milk or milk and water. Simmer gently for 8 minutes. Meanwhile, chop watercress finely, reserving a few sprigs for garnish. Add watercress to soup after 5 minutes with lemon juice and seasoning. When the 8 minutes is up, check seasoning, liquidize, then pour soup into bowls, garnishing each serving with a few watercress sprigs.

Gazpacho

A Spanish chilled soup that has many variations, and is extremely quick to make, if you have a blender.

(Serves 4 — about 105 calories each.)

Imperial (Metric)
2 slices of wholemeal bread
1 tablespoonful olive oil
1 clove garlic
1 green pepper
8 oz (225g) ripe tomatoes
¼ cucumber
¾ pint (450ml) tomato juice
1 tablespoonful wine vinegar
1 small onion
Sea salt and black pepper

American
2 slices of wholemeal bread
1 tablespoonful + 1 teaspoonful
  olive oil
1 clove garlic
1 green pepper
2 cupsful ripe tomatoes
¼ cucumber
2 cupsful tomato juice
1 tablespoonful + 1 teaspoonful
  wine vinegar
1 small onion
Sea salt and black pepper

Dice the bread and toss in a frying pan lightly brushed with oil. Peel the garlic clove and de-seed the pepper. Wash the tomatoes and cucumber but do not peel. Liquidize all but 1 tomato, the tomato juice, olive oil, vinegar, half the onion, and half the cucumber. Adjust taste with sea salt, pepper and a little lemon juice if liked.

Chop tomato, remaining onion, cucumber and green pepper finely and add to soup, or as in Spain, serve in separate little bowls for people to add themselves. Make another bowl for the *croûtons* or add to soup as you serve.

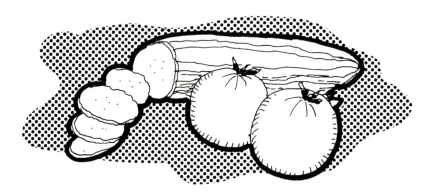

Courgette and tarragon soup

(Serves 4 — about 85 calories each, using ½ pint/300ml skim milk.)

Imperial (Metric)	**American**
1 teaspoonful vegetable oil	1 teaspoonful vegetable oil
1 onion	1 onion
1 lb (450g) courgettes	3 cupsful zucchini
1¼ pint (750ml) stock or stock and milk mixture	3 cupsful stock or stock and milk mixture
1 teaspoonful dried tarragon	1 teaspoonful dried tarragon
Sea salt and black pepper	Sea salt and black pepper
4 tablespoonsful natural yogurt	4 heaping tablespoonsful natural yogurt

Heat oil in thick-based saucepan, turn sliced onion for a few minutes. Add sliced courgettes (zucchini) and stock, simmer for about 8 minutes. Liquidize with tarragon and seasoning. Pour into bowls and stir a tablespoonful of yogurt into each bowl. Garnish with *croûtons* or parsley if liked. Serve hot or cold.

Variations: this is an example of the *purée* method, and can be used just as well with carrots, which should be finely grated for speedy cooking, or with parsnips, which will take a few minutes longer.

Instead of using tarragon, you could curry these soups by turning a large teaspoonful of curry powder or garam masala in the oil with the onion — this releases the aromatic oils which carry the curry flavours.

Cooked rice or beans could be added to the soup at the end, just warmed through.

Cream of mushroom soup

You can make this soup just as well with mushroom stalks, which can often be bought far cheaper than whole mushrooms.

(Serves 4 — about 180 calories each.)

Imperial (Metric)

1½ oz (45g) vegetable oil or soft margarine

8 oz (225g) mushrooms or stalks, washed but not peeled

1½ oz (45g) wholemeal plain flour

1 pint (600ml) half stock, half skim milk

1 bay leaf

Handful of parsley

2 level tablespoonsful skim dried milk

Sea salt and black pepper

Lemon juice to taste

American

2½ tablespoonsful vegetable oil or soft margarine

4 cupsful mushrooms or stalks, washed but not peeled

4 tablespoonsful wholemeal plain flour

2½ cupsful half stock, half skim milk

1 bay leaf

Handful of parsley

2 rounded tablespoonsful skim dried milk

Sea salt and black pepper

Lemon juice to taste

Dip a pastry brush in the oil or margarine, and use to wipe round a thick-based frying pan (skillet). Heat this pan, and tip in roughly chopped mushrooms or stalks. Turn heat down low. In separate saucepan, slowly heat the remaining fat, the flour and the stock and milk which you have previously whizzed until smooth in blender. Add bay leaf to pan, and stir constantly so that as boiling point is reached, mixture thickens smoothly. If not, return mixture to liquidizer for a few seconds to blend. Simmer over a low heat for a minute or two, then add mushrooms from frying pan, extract bay leaf and blend again, adding parsley, skim milk powder and seasoning. Taste and add lemon juice to your liking. Reheat if necessary and serve.

Variations: spinach soup can be made by exactly the same method, but lightly cooking spinach leaves in just the water clinging to them after washing. *Purée* spinach, then add to flour and milk mixture as you would fried mushrooms.

Sweetcorn soup can be made in the same way, or if using frozen or tinned kernels, simply by adding 8 oz (225g)/1 cupful to soup for final blending stage, then reheating soup. Instead of lemon juice, a little cayenne pepper goes well here.

Salads

Salads are one of the quickest kinds of meal to make — as well as one of the best to eat. Richer in vitamins, minerals and some kinds of fibre than most meals, they also offer all this goodness and flavour for rather few calories.

If you think salads are not high enough in protein for a meal, it may mean you are imagining plates of lettuce and tomatoes. But if you widen your salad-making ideas to the more satisfying salads based on the list of ingredients below, you'll be getting enough 'solid' food to give you plenty of protein. You'll also find that you look forward much more to salads, even in cold weather, as a satisfying meal.

The essence of quick salads is good cutting equipment. If you are fast with a sharp knife, you can probably rely mainly on that and a grater. The easiest graters are either a really solid stainless steel square one, which gives you a solid base to press down; or a *Mouli Legumes*, which comes with a variety of discs for a choice of slices and shredding thicknesses. See also the notes on equipment, page 17.

Salad Ingredients

Apples*
Artichokes, globe and Jerusalem
Asparagus
Beans — green, broad (Windsor)
   or cooked dried varieties
Beansprouts — bought or home-
   grown (see Thinking Ahead)
Beetroot (beet) — raw or cooked
Broccoli
Brussels sprouts
Cabbage
Carrots
Cauliflower
Celery
Chick peas (garbanzos)
Chicory
Chinese 'leaves' (cabbage)
Cucumber
Dandelion leaves, very young

Endive ('curly lettuce')
Kohlrabi
Leeks
Lentils, cooked
Lettuce
Mangetout (snow peas)
Mushrooms*
Mustard and cress
Onions, large and spring (scallions)
Parsnips
Peas
Peppers, red and green
Potatoes, cooked
Spinach
Swedes (rutabagas)
Tomatoes
Turnips
Watercress

These are mainly low-calorie, high-vitamin and mineral foods. The exceptions are the beans, lentils and peas, which in addition provide a substantial amount of protein, and more fibre.

To make a complete main dish from a salad, you need to include one or more of these, or of the following:

Cheese — soft or hard.
Eggs — hard-boiled or slices of omelette.
Fish — fresh, smoked or tinned.
Meat
Nuts
Peanuts
Seeds — pumpkin, sunflower or sesame.
Whole grains — cooked brown rice, barley grains, bulgur wheat, rye grains or flaked versions.
Wholemeal pasta — macaroni lengths, shells or twists.
Wholemeal bread or rolls, eaten with salad.
Lentil, pea or bean soup, eaten with the salad.

These add protein — and calories. They should be in smaller amounts than the fresh vegetables, especially if you use the higher-fat items, that is, hard or cream cheese, oily fish such as mackerel, nuts and peanuts or seeds. Meat should be as lean as possible. Yogurt and soft cheese dressings also add protein.

Many people like the 'sweet and sour' flavour given to salads by adding fruit. Here are some fruity or other unusual additions:

Avocado pears**	Dates	Pears
Bananas*	Grapes	Pineapple
Bran	Herbs	Prunes
Chestnuts (cooked)	Oranges	Wheatgerm
Coconut, desiccated	Olives	

* All these ingredients must be tossed in lemon juice as soon as they are cut, or they will go brown and quickly lose their colour and texture, turning black and soft.
** Not such an unusual salad ingredient, but noted here because although it is a vegetable, it is very high in fat and thence in calories too.

Salad Combinations
Although there are some classic salads, such as Waldorf (diced apple, chopped celery and walnuts), there are no rules for making a good salad mixture. Literally hundreds of different combinations of the above ingredients make delicious eating.

There are, however, rules about dressing salads. Most root vegetable, bean, grain and fish ingredients benefit from being dressed as soon as they are cut: otherwise, they tend to dry out and become unappetizing. Leafy green ingredients, in contrast, should not be dressed until a few minutes before they are eaten. If dressed too early, they will wilt and lose all their crispness. A few salad recipes do this on purpose, as some people enjoy the result: try it using the recipe for Wilted Lettuce Salad below.

In addition to the variety of salad ingredients, how you cut the vegetables also opens up more room for different results: some people like chunks to eat in their fingers, or dip in savoury mixtures. Some like the vegetables chopped very small indeed. In between, you can shred carrots or cabbage finely or coarsely, slice sprouts or leeks thinly or roughly, or cut all your ingredients into dice or matchstick shapes.

Here are some tried and tested favourites to set you off:

Coleslaw: thinly shredded carrot and white cabbage, perhaps with finely sliced onion too. Add a handful of raisins and some peanuts if liked. Dress with dressing nos. 2, 3 or 4 from Useful Extras.

Greek: large slices of tomato, cucumber, onion, with black olives and small pieces of Greek 'feta' cheese (English Cheshire is probably the nearest equivalent). Olive oil dressing.

Nicoise: quartered tomatoes, lightly cooked green beans, black olives, anchovies, hard-boiled egg in quarters, and tuna fish. Dressing no. 4.

Tabbouleh: put bulgur wheat in a sieve (about 1 cupful — only fill sieve half full) and run under the tap thoroughly. Leave to drain — it will quickly expand (in about 30 minutes). Mix with a whole bunch of chopped parsley, finely chopped onion and dressing no. 4.

Orange slices, watercress and black olives. Dressing no. 4.

Gayelord Hauser's Finger Salad: 'Tender carrot sticks, bits of raw cauliflower, slices of green and red peppers; red and white radishes; young onions and celery, whole small tomatoes.' To serve with vegetable salt or chilled dressing no. 3, or a favourite dip.

Mushrooms, sliced, with plenty of chopped parsley, tossed in lemon juice.

Caesar Salad: Crisp lettuce, torn into pieces, chopped anchovy fillets, grated

Parmesan cheese and chopped poached or scrambled egg. Wholemeal bread diced and made into *croûtons* by frying in oil flavoured with a crushed clove of garlic. Dressing no. 4.

Three-bean Salad: lightly cooked or tender raw green beans, mixed with cooked red kidney beans and cooked haricot beans. Could also be made deliciously with chick peas (garbanzo beans), butter beans (Lima beans) or flageolets (which have a lovely pale green colour). Dressing nos. 2 or 4.

Wilted Lettuce Salad: the soft-leaved kind of lettuce, torn in pieces and mixed with chopped spring onions (scallions). Pour over per head of lettuce: 3 tablespoonsful vinegar, 3 tablespoonsful raw cane sugar and 3 tablespoonsful mayonnaise that have been heated together (*not* boiled, or mayonnaise will curdle). Serve immediately, with *croûtons* if liked.

Russian Salad: one of the most abused salads of all time, this does not have to be bland cubes of anonymous vegetables, drowned in salad dressing in the tin. Good Russian salad is better made from lightly cooked large pieces of carrot, potato, swede (rutabaga), turnip and/or parsnip, which are then diced, mixed with raw or lightly cooked peas and lightly dressed with nos. 1 or 2.

Brown rice, toasted peanuts, chopped green or red peppers, celery, broad beans (Windsor beans) or peas, and watercress. Leave the last item out until just serving, so that you can dress the rice earlier, with no. 2 or 4.

Watercress, Chinese cabbage and lots of roughly chopped parsley makes a nicely different green salad — as would cucumber (unpeeled) slices, shredded spinach (uncooked) and mangetout (snow peas), lightly cooked. Dressing no. 4.

Chicory with cubed apple and cooked beetroot, dressed with yogurt and lemon juice (add beetroot/beet just before serving, or it will stain the whole salad pink). For a main course salad, cubes of cheese go well with this one.

California platter

The kind of platter you find along the sunny coast of California can be varied to use seasonal and favourite ingredients. The two essential ingredients are lavish quantities — the plate must look generous — and neat arrangement which turns this from a fancy salad into a mouth-watering eyeful.

(Serves 4 — about 350 calories each.)

Imperial (Metric)	**American**
1 lb (450g) cottage cheese	2 cupsful cottage cheese
2 oz (50g) hazelnuts or almond flakes	½ cupful hazelnuts or almond flakes
1 orange, segmented	1 orange, segmented
1 grapefruit, segmented	1 grapefruit, segmented
1 lb (450g) black grapes	3 cupsful black grapes
2 kiwi fruit	2 kiwi fruit
2 pears	2 pears
3 peaches	3 peaches
1 large apple	1 large apple
2 bananas	2 bananas

Using an ice cream scoop if available, divide cottage cheese into four mounds in the centre of large dinner plates. Toast nuts in dry frying pan over a gentle heat for a few minutes, until browning. Slice all the fruit neatly, leaving banana and apple until last: these will brown unless eaten within 15 minutes or tossed in a little lemon or apple juice. Arrange fruit slices in overlapping 'spokes' round plate. Sprinkle nuts over salad, together with some cinnamon if liked.

Note: do not peel pears, apple, peaches or grapes.

Whole-meal muesli

The original muesli recipe devised by Dr Bircher-Benner, to be eaten as a complete fruit meal. The only change is that he suggested soaking the oats overnight. You can speed things up by using rolled oats with hot water.

(Serves 2 — about 230 calories each.)

Imperial (Metric)
2 tablespoonsful rolled oats or
   muesli base
1 lemon or orange
2 large or 4 small apples
2 tablespoonsful nuts, whole or
   freshly chopped
2 tablespoonsful natural yogurt or
   top-of-the-milk
Optional: more fresh fruit, roughly
   chopped; 1 large tablespoonful
   raisins, currants or sultanas

American
2 heaped tablespoonsful rolled
   oats or muesli base
1 lemon or orange
2 large or 4 small apples
2 heaped tablespoonsful nuts,
   whole or freshly chopped
2 heaped tablespoonsful natural
   yogurt or top-of-the-milk
Optional: more fresh fruit, roughly
   chopped; 1 large tablespoonful
   raisins, currants or golden
   seedless raisins

Place oats and dried fruit used in heat-resistant bowl. Just cover with hot but not boiling water, stirring to mix. Leave to stand while you squeeze juice from lemon, or chop up orange. Add to oats with grated apple, nuts and yogurt, plus extra fruit of any kind.

Allow to stand for several minutes, so that the oats can swell fully, making this dish much tastier and more satisfying.

The main course sauce

We are all used to the idea of a cheese sauce turning a vegetable or grain into a main dish — as in cauliflower cheese and macaroni cheese.

Here are three variations on that theme, with less usual sauces that are substantial enough both in flavour and protein to make a meal out of whatever green and root vegetables you have to hand.

When your sauce is simmering, cook a generous amount of vegetables in a mean amount of water. Cover tightly and allow them to cook only until they're tender, not mushy.

Peanut sauce

(Serves 4 — about 210 calories each.)

Imperial (Metric)	American
1 medium onion	1 medium onion
3 tomatoes	3 tomatoes
5 oz (175g) shelled unsalted peanuts	1¼ cupsful shelled unsalted peanuts
8 fl oz (250ml) water	1 cupful water
1 teaspoonful sea salt	1 teaspoonful sea salt
½ teaspoonful dried mixed herbs or 1 teaspoonful fresh	½ teaspoonful dried mixed herbs or 1 teaspoonful fresh

Sweat finely chopped onion and tomatoes in a little vegetable oil for 4 minutes. Meanwhile, grind peanuts and mix with a little of the water to make a paste. Add to tomato mixture. Add remaining water, salt and herbs, bring to the boil stirring, and simmer gently for a few minutes before serving. Liquidize if you wish for a smoother texture.

Hope Price, Loughton, Essex

Curried nut sauce

(Serves 4 — about 190 calories each.)

Imperial (Metric)	American
1 cupful ground nuts	1 cupful ground nuts
½ pint (300ml) skim milk	1¼ cupsful skim milk
4 oz (100g) chopped mushrooms	2 cupsful chopped mushrooms
½ teaspoonful curry powder	½ teaspoonful curry powder
1 onion, chopped finely	1 onion, chopped finely
1 tablespoonful chopped parsley	1 large tablespoonful chopped parsley
Sea salt and black pepper	Sea salt and black pepper

Mix nuts, milk, mushrooms, curry powder and onion using blender if available. Cook together over low heat for a few minutes until the mixture thickens, stirring often. Add parsley and seasoning before serving.

Tahini ★

A creamy sauce widely used in Middle Eastern cooking, tahini can be served thick and cold as a dip, or heated to turn a vegetable platter into satisfying main dish. The spread is rich in calcium from the sesame seeds, as well as providing protein, a lot of unsaturated oil and fibre. It can also be used as a sandwich spread with salad, or to add extra flavour to plainly cooked fish.

(Makes 1 jar — about 1800 calories in total.)

Imperial (Metric)	American
8 oz (225g) toasted sesame seeds	2 cupsful toasted sesame seeds
4 tablespoonsful olive oil, cold-pressed if possible	5 tablespoonsful olive oil, cold-pressed if possible
2 cloves garlic, crushed	2 cloves garlic, crushed
Juice of 2 lemons	Juice of 2 lemons
½ teaspoonful coriander seed	½ teaspoonful coriander seed
½ teaspoonful sea salt	½ teaspoonful sea salt

Use a blender if possible, placing all ingredients in goblet with a little water if mixture is too dry for the machine. Blend until creamy. To make tahini by hand, a ridged Japanese mortar, called a *suribachi*, is custom-built. You can find these in many wholefood stores. It is important that the sesame seeds are crushed, or the flavour won't come out. This mixture will keep well. To dilute its rich oil content, you may like to blend it with soft cheese, low- or medium-fat kinds, as you use it: dilute it about 2 parts of tahini to 1 of soft cheese. If you add the soft cheese when you make it, you must use the spread within a week and keep it in the refrigerator.

Twenty Minute Main Courses

Fish chowder ✓

You don't have to skin fish for this recipe. You can use any smoked or white fish — cod, haddock, whiting or coley. By the way, the grey tint of raw coley turns a more attractive white when it cooks.

(Serves 4 — about 195 calories each.)

Imperial (Metric)
1 oz (25g) butter or soft margarine
1 small onion, finely sliced
2 sticks of celery, chopped
1 small red or green pepper
1 medium potato, diced
1 clove garlic (optional), crushed
¼ pint (150ml) fish or other stock
12 oz (325g) fish
¼ pint (150ml) skim milk
1 flat tablespoonful (15g) cornflour
Sea salt and black pepper
Generous handful of parsley

American
¼ cupful butter or soft margarine
1 small onion, finely sliced
2 sticks of celery, chopped
1 small red or green pepper
1 medium potato, diced
1 clove garlic (optional), crushed
½ cupful plus 1 tablespoonful fish
   or other stock
12 ounces fish
1 cupful + 1 tablespoonful skim
   milk
1 rounded tablespoonful
   cornstarch
Sea salt and black pepper
Generous handful of parsley

Melt the butter or margarine in a large saucepan. *Sauté* the onion, celery, pepper, potato and garlic if using. Add the stock, then simmer until potatoes are just tender — about 10 minutes. Add the fish, cut into cubes. Blend the milk and cornflour to a smooth paste, add to pan and simmer for 5 minutes. Season and serve with lots of roughly chopped parsley mixed in.

Sesame patties

Once you have a nut grater, coffee mill, food processor or electric coffee grinder, this is a very quick recipe indeed.

(Serves 4-5, about 380 or 304 calories each.)

Imperial (Metric)	**American**
1 medium onion	1 medium onion
1 clove garlic (optional)	1 clove garlic (optional)
1 teaspoonful vegetable oil	1 teaspoonful vegetable oil
3 oz (75g) grated hazelnuts	¾ cupful grated hazelnuts
3 oz (75g) grated walnuts	¾ cupful English walnuts
3 oz (75g) wholemeal breadcrumbs	1 ½ cupsful wholemeal breadcrumbs
1 teaspoonful oregano or basil	1 teaspoonful oregano or basil
Good pinch of mixed herbs	Good pinch of mixed herbs
1 egg	1 egg
About 2 oz (50g) sesame seeds, crushed	½ cupful sesame seeds, crushed

Finely chop or grate onion, crush garlic and turn over low heat in the oil for 5 minutes. Meanwhile, grate and mix nuts, breadcrumbs and herbs. Add onion, garlic and egg. Check seasoning, adding a little salt or soya/tamari sauce if too bland and a little milk if mixture is too crumbly. Divide mixture into four or five large patties, roll in sesame seeds to cover. Grill under medium heat for about 6-8 minutes, turning once. Serve as hamburgers.

Note: to crush sesame seeds, put in coffee mill for a few seconds, or use an old-fashioned pestle and mortar, or a *suribachi*, the ridged Japanese pottery mortar which they use for the job.

Stuffed tomatoes

(Serves 4 — about 290 calories each.)

Imperial (Metric)
8 large tomatoes
8 oz (225g) fresh wholemeal
  breadcrumbs
8 oz (225g) cottage cheese
2 heaped tablespoonsful flaked
  almonds
Rind and juice of 1 lemon

American
8 large tomatoes
4¼ cupsful fresh wholemeal
  breadcrumbs
1 cupful cottage cheese
3 tablespoonsful flaked almonds
Rind and juice of 1 lemon

Heat oven to 425°F/220°C (Gas Mark 7). Halve tomatoes horizontally, and scoop out centres. Mash with all other ingredients, and pile on shells in flat, lightly oiled oven-proof dish. Cover with lid or foil. Bake for 15 minutes. If preferred, use sunflower seeds or chopped walnuts (English walnuts) instead of almonds, and sprinkle on top of mixture to garnish. Don't worry if the shells will not hold all the mixture: the extra can look attractive if spread around baking dish.

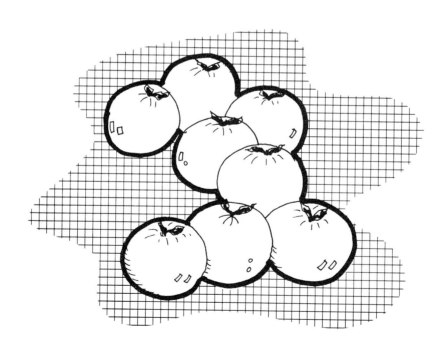

Spaghetti 'Marinara'

A basic spaghetti which you can vary, if you prefer, with more cheese, cooked mushrooms, or other flavours. Cook two batches of sauce, and you'll have a good filling for pitta bread, a ready-made pizza topping or a tasty baked flan filling.

(Serves 4 — about 320 calories each.)

Imperial (Metric)	American
8 oz (225g) wholewheat spaghetti	8 ounces wholewheat spaghetti
1 large onion	1 large onion
1 tablespoonful vegetable oil, preferably cold-pressed	1 tablespoonful vegetable oil, preferably cold-pressed
1 clove garlic (optional)	1 clove garlic (optional)
5-6 tomatoes or 1 × 14 oz (400g) tin	2 cupsful tomatoes or 1 × 14 oz tin
2 teaspoonsful Worcestershire sauce	2 teaspoonsful Worcestershire sauce
1 teaspoonful yeast extract or vegetable flavouring	1 teaspoonful yeast extract or vegetable flavouring
¼ pint (150ml) water	½ cupful + 2 tablespoonsful water
1 level tablespoonful cornflour	1 rounded tablespoonful cornstarch
½ teaspoonful sea salt	½ teaspoonful sea salt
Freshly ground black pepper	Freshly ground black pepper
2 teaspoonsful chopped fresh or 1 teaspoonful dried basil	2 teaspoonsful chopped fresh or 1 teaspoonful dried basil
Handful of parsley, chopped	Handful of parsley, chopped
1 oz (25g) grated Parmesan or Cheddar cheese	¼ cupful grated Parmesan or Cheddar cheese

Set the spaghetti to boil in a big pan of unsalted boiling water. Set a timer for 12 minutes. Chop the onion finely and turn in the oil for about 5 minutes, adding crushed garlic after 3 minutes if using. Add tomatoes and sauce. Blend yeast or stock powder with a little of the water and cornflour (cornstarch). Then mix with remaining water and add to the pan with salt and pepper. Bring to the boil and simmer for 10 minutes. Add basil and parsley. When spaghetti's 12 minutes are up, check for done-ness: it won't get as soft as white spaghetti; nor will it go soggy or need rinsing. Drain, mix with the sauce, sprinkle with the grated cheese and serve immediately.

French onion soup ✓

(Serves 4 as starter, 2 as meal — about 115 or 230 calories each, 10 or 20 extra
with sherry or port.)

Imperial (Metric)

2 large onions
1 clove garlic, crushed (optional)
1 tablespoonful vegetable oil or
    soft vegetable margarine
1 pint water or stock
Bay leaf
1 large teaspoonful yeast extract
1 slice of wholemeal bread
2 oz (50g) mature Cheddar cheese

American

2 large onions
1 clove garlic, crushed (optional)
1 large tablespoonful vegetable oil
    or soft vegetable margarine
3¼ cupsful water or stock
Bay leaf
1 large teaspoonful yeast extract
1 slice of wholemeal bread
¼ cupful mature Cheddar cheese

Optional: 1 clove garlic, crushed; 1 tablespoonful sherry or port.

Peel onions and slice very thinly. Heat fat in thick-based saucepan, and cook
onion and garlic if using gently for about 5 minutes until it is soft. Pour over water
or stock, adding bay leaf and yeast extract. Simmer gently for about 10 minutes.
Meanwhile, toast bread and cut into cubes. Divide between soup bowls and
sprinkle with the cheese, grated. Check soup seasoning, and remove bay leaf.
Pour over bread and cheese. Stir a teaspoonful of port or sherry, if using, into
each bowl.

Lightning lentils

A quick protein dish to serve with green vegetables, or over pasta.

(Serves 4 — about 200 calories each.)

Imperial (Metric)	American
8 oz (225g) split red lentils	1 ¼ cupsful split red lentils
1 bay leaf	1 bay leaf
1 onion	1 onion
1 teaspoonful vegetable oil	1 teaspoonful vegetable oil
4 oz (100g) mushrooms	2 cupsful mushrooms
1 clove garlic (optional)	1 clove garlic (optional)
Sea salt and black pepper	Sea salt and black pepper

Rinse lentils under tap in sieve. Place in pan with two large cups of water and the bay leaf. Bring to the boil, turn to lowest heat and cover to simmer for 15 minutes.

Meanwhile, slice onion and 'sweat' in oil for about 10 minutes, covered over low heat. Add sliced mushrooms and garlic if using for 5 minutes more. Test lentils after 15 minutes, and if done, season and stir in the green vegetables. Otherwise, simmer 5 minutes more before adding vegetables and seasoning. Lentils should come out dry and fluffy. If they are too wet, simmer longer with lid off pan. If too dry, add a little more water.

To change this dish into a soup, simply add more water, stock or milk at the end, and whizz to fine texture in blender with a generous handful of parsley.

Tuna macaroni

A 15-minute dinner!

(Serves 4 — about 380 calories each.)

Imperial (Metric)	American
8 oz (225g) wholemeal macaroni	1 ⅔ cupsful wholemeal macaroni
1 large onion, sliced thin	1 large onion, sliced thin
½ oz (15g) oil from the fish or other	1 tablespoonful oil from the fish or other
½ teaspoonful mixed herbs	½ teaspoonful mixed herbs
1 tablespoonful tomato *purée*	1 rounded tablespoonsful tomato paste
1 tin (200g) tuna fish	1 cupful tuna fish
14 oz (400g) tomatoes or 1 tin	2 cupsful tomatoes or 1 tin
Sea salt and black pepper	Sea salt and black pepper

Optional extras: sliced mushrooms, peas, cooked vegetables.

Boil macaroni in lots of unsalted water, for 10-12 minutes, until just tender. Meanwhile, gently cook onion in the oil for 5 minutes, then add all other ingredients. Season and serve stirred into macaroni lengths.

Variation: vegetarians can add cubes of nutmeat, or walnut (English walnut) halves, in place of the tuna.

Fish pie

(Serves 4 — about 280 calories each.)

Imperial (Metric)
1 lb (450g) potatoes
½ oz (15g) butter or soft margarine
½ oz (15g) wholemeal plain flour
¼ pint (150ml) skim milk
1 lb (450g) any white or smoked fish
8 oz (225g) peas, broad beans or spinach
Sea salt and black pepper
½ teaspoonful mustard powder

American
3 cupsful, potatoes, diced roughly
3 teaspoonsful butter or soft margarine
6 teaspoonsful wholemeal plain flour
½ cupful + 1 tablespoonful skim milk
1 pound any white or smoked fish
3 cupsful peas, Windsor beans or spinach
Sea salt and black pepper
½ teaspoonful mustard powder

Set saucepan with 1½ in. of water to boil. Chop unpeeled potatoes into small chunks for quick boiling, put in water as you prepare them. Place fish in saucepan or frying pan (skillet) with enough hot water to just cover and gently poach for 5 minutes. Drain and flake fish from skin, removing any bones. While fish is poaching cook chosen vegetables in minimum of boiling water. Drain. Heat grill. Place fat in saucepan and stir in flour over low heat to make thick paste. Gradually add milk, stirring all the time to prevent lumps forming in the sauce. Stir fish and vegetables into sauce and simmer, stirring for about 5 minutes until heated through. Transfer to heatproof dish and place, covered, under grill. Drain and mash potatoes with a little skim milk and spread over fish. Return to grill to brown or heat through, if necessary. Garnish with cayenne pepper and parsley.

Fish cakes

Fish cakes do not have to be deep-fried or even fried at all — they can be grilled or baked, for less fat and less fiddling.

Use the fishmonger's best bargain — here's your chance to use huss, scad, or that frightening-faced John Dory. Flaked into fish cakes, no one will know the difference.

(Serves 4 — about 180 calories each.)

Imperial (Metric)	American
8 oz (225g) potatoes	8 ounces potatoes
8 oz (225g) fish, preferably white variety	8 ounces fish, preferably white variety
½ oz (15g) soft vegetable margarine	1 tablespoonful soft vegetable margarine
1 egg, beaten	1 egg, beaten
1 small onion, finely chopped	1 small onion, finely chopped
2 teaspoonsful tomato *purée*	2 teaspoonsful tomato paste
½ oz (15g) parsley	Handful parsley
½ teaspoonful sea salt and black pepper	½ teaspoonful sea salt and black pepper
1½ oz (45g) wholemeal breadcrumbs	⅓ cupful wholemeal breadcrumbs
1 lemon	1 lemon

Wash and cube potato and cook in small amount of boiling water. Slice fish and add to potatoes after 10 minutes. Simmer together for 5 minutes. Meanwhile mix half the egg, onion, *purée*, salt and pepper. Drain fish and potatoes and remove skin and bones from fish. Mash potatoes with margarine. Add fish and egg mixture to potatoes and mix thoroughly. Shape into fishcakes (adding some of the breadcrumbs if mixture is too soft) and dip in remaining egg which will make breadcrumbs adhere. Lightly oil a frying pan (skillet) and cook for a few minutes, turning once, or place in grill pan and toast under grill or bake for few minutes in oven.

Vulgar bulgur

Bulgur is a kind of cracked wheat which has been par-boiled when you buy it — hence its speed in cooking. You can make this recipe in the same length of time using millet or buckwheat instead.

(Serves 4 generously — about 380 calories each, if using peas, sweetcorn or broad beans/Windsor beans; slightly less for the other vegetables listed.)

Imperial (Metric)
1 onion
4 oz (100g) whole hazelnuts
1 teaspoonful vegetable oil
8 oz (225g) bulgur wheat
1 pint (600ml) stock
1 tablespoonful soya or tamari
  sauce
2 teaspoonsful fresh herbs or 1
  teaspoonful dried herbs
At least one of these: 1 cupful of
  peas, sweetcorn, cooked beans,
  cauliflower, sprouts, courgettes,
  broad or green beans, or fennel.
Sea salt and black pepper

American
1 onion
1 cupful whole hazelnuts
1 teaspoonful vegetable oil
1¼ cupsful bulgur wheat
2½ cupsful stock
1 large tablespoonful soya or
  tamari sauce
2 teaspoonsful fresh or 1 dried
  herbs
At least one of these: 1 cupful of
  peas, sweetcorn, cooked beans,
  cauliflower, sprouts, zucchini,
  Windsor or green beans, or
  fennel
Sea salt and black pepper

Grate onion and turn with the nuts in the oil for 5 minutes. Then rinse bulgur in sieve under tap, add to onion and nuts, turn together and add the stock, soya/tamari and herbs. Bring to the boil, cover and simmer for 15 minutes. Meanwhile, lightly cook your cupful of vegetables (or several cupsful), chopping courgettes (zucchini), beans or fennel coarsely.

After 15 minutes, add vegetables to bulgur mixture, fluff up, check seasoning and serve as you would risotto.

Fish burgers ✓

An unusual combination with macaroni — serve in brown buns and let McDonalds eat their heart out! This is also a very economical meal. Any fresh fish can be used, but white kinds look best.

(Serves 4 — about 340 calories each, or 320 using white fish.)

Imperial (Metric)	American
3 oz (75g) wholemeal macaroni	⅔ cupful wholemeal macaroni
8 oz (225g) fish	8 ounces fish
1 ½ oz (45g) soft vegetable margarine	2 tablespoonsful soft vegetable margarine
1 ½ oz (45g) wholemeal plain flour	4 tablespoonsful wholemeal plain flour
8 fl oz (250ml) stock from cooking fish or skim milk	1 cupful stock from cooking fish or skim milk
Pinch of mustard powder	Pinch of mustard powder
1 ½ oz (45g) Cheddar cheese, grated	⅓ cupful Cheddar cheese, grated
Sea salt and black pepper	Sea salt and black pepper

For coating

½ oz (15g) wholemeal plain flour	2 tablespoonsful wholemeal plain flour
About ½ egg, beaten	About ½ egg, beaten
1 oz (25g) wholemeal breadcrumbs	¼ cupful wholemeal breadcrumbs

Boil macaroni briskly in plenty of unsalted water for 10 minutes. Meanwhile, poach fish in enough water to cover for barely 5 minutes. While this cooks, melt margarine over a low heat and stir in the flour. Remove pan from heat, gradually work in 8 fl oz (250ml, 1 cupful) of cooking water from fish, making up quantity wish skim milk if necessary. Return mixture to cooker (stove) when smooth, and reheat slowly, stirring steadily until it thickens. Simmer for a few minutes and remove from heat. Flake fish from skin, removing bones and stir in with drained macaroni, mustard, cheese and seasoning. Add fish mixture to sauce and mix thoroughly. Shape into flat burgers, using a little flour if necessary. Dip in the beaten egg (you won't need all the egg), then in breadcrumbs before grilling for a few minutes on each side. These can be frozen and then cooked without thawing.

Spinach roll

An excellent main course that meat-eaters will enjoy as much as vegetarians, partly because it looks very special.

(Serves 4-6 — about 295 or 197 calories per portion.)

Imperial (Metric)	American
1 onion, finely chopped	1 onion, finely chopped
1 oz (25g) butter or soft vegetable margarine	¼ cupful butter or soft vegetable margarine
12 oz (325g) fresh spinach	1 pound fresh spinach
1 large tablespoonful wholemeal flour	1 heaped tablespoonful wholemeal flour
¼ pint (150ml) skim milk	½ cupful + 1 tablespoonful skim milk
Sea salt and black pepper	Sea salt and black pepper
3 free-range eggs, separated	3 free-range eggs, separated

Filling

8 oz (225g, 1 cupful) cottage cheese or low-fat soft curd cheese *or* 4 oz (100g, 2 cupsful) mushrooms, sliced and *sautéed* in 2 teaspoonsful vegetable oil

Lightly oil Swiss roll tin and line with greaseproof or parchment paper, then oil again.

Sauté onion in butter or margarine for 5 minutes. Wash spinach leaves and place in saucepan. Cover and simmer for 4 minutes. Drain excess water to use as stock. Liquidize spinach briefly. Drain again, if necessary. Heat oven to 375°F/190°C (Gas Mark 5). Add flour to *sautéd* onion and stir over low heat. Gradually stir in spinach stock and milk to obtain a thick sauce. Remove from heat and season. Beat in egg yolks one at a time. Add spinach to mixture.

Whisk egg whites until firm enough to hold peaks and fold into the spinach mixture. Pour into prepared tin and bake for 12-15 minutes, until firm to touch. While cooking prepare filling and warm a serving dish.

When spinach roll is cooked remove from tin and place upside-down on a sheet of greaseproof paper on a flat work surface. Peel off paper and spread with cheese or mushrooms. Using the piece of paper beneath the roll to support it carefully roll up, working away from you. Place the roll, wrapped in the paper, on warmed plate allowing it to rest for a minute to set in position. Remove paper and serve.

Savoury swiss roll

Looks fancy, easier than it looks — that's the appeal of this interesting dish. Vary the stuffing according to what you have handy for an emergency dish that is also a good dinner party one.

(Serves 4 — about 230 calories each with vegetable filling.)

Imperial (Metric)	American
For roll	
3 eggs	3 eggs
4 oz (100g) wholemeal plain flour	1 cupful wholemeal plain flour
2 teaspoonsful baking powder	2 teaspoonsful baking powder
Sea salt, mustard and black pepper	Sea salt, mustard and black pepper
1 tablespoonful vegetable oil	1 ½ tablespoonsful vegetable oil
2 tablespoonsful hot water	3 tablespoonsful hot water
For filling	
4 oz (100g) low-fat soft cheese	½ cupful low-fat soft cheese

blended with: 1 finely chopped bunch of watercress *or* 4 oz (100g, ½ cupful) finely chopped, well-drained, lightly cooked spinach *or* 4 oz (100g, 2 cupsful) sliced, *sautéed* mushrooms *or* 4 oz (100g, 1 cupful) sliced, *sautéed* courgettes (zucchini). The filling can be further flavoured with peanut butter, chopped nuts, chopped hard-boiled eggs. Flaked cooked fish can also be worked into the cheese.

Pre-heat oven to 400°F/200°C (Gas Mark 6). Whip eggs in electric mixer or over a pan of hot water until light and thick. Sift flour, retaining bran in sieve, with baking powder, salt, a little powdered mustard and pepper. Fold flour into the egg mixture followed by oil and water, mixed together.

Line and then grease a Swiss roll tin. Pour in mixture, bake until springy for about 10-12 minutes. Transfer roll, with paper still underneath, to a clean worktop. Spread filling evenly over roll. Now with a narrow side towards you, make cut half way through roll about 1 in. from your end. This helps the first part of the rolling tuck in neatly. Roll up, using paper to keep roll intact and even, detaching paper as you roll away from you. Leave tucked in cloth for a minute before serving.

Note: filling should be fairly moist.

Ferial Rogers

Thirty Minute Main Courses

Little cheese - nut savouries

(Serves 4 — about 260 calories each.)

Imperial (Metric)
4 large eggs
½ teaspoonful sea salt
8 oz (225g) cottage cheese
2 oz (50g) almonds, roughly
   chopped
1 oz (25g) sultanas or stoned raisins
Paprika pepper to garnish

American
4 large eggs
½ teaspoonful sea salt
1 cupful cottage cheese
½ cupful almonds, roughly
   chopped
¼ cupful golden seedless raisins or
   stoned raisins
Paprika pepper to garnish

Boil a kettle of water. Pre-heat oven to 375°F/190°C (Gas Mark 5). Beat eggs and stir in all the remaining ingredients except paprika. Divide into four lightly oiled ramekins. Set in dish of boiling water and bake for about 20 minutes, or until set. Serve in ramekins garnished with a little paprika, or turn out.

   Note: you don't need to wait until the oven is hot.

   Variations: any kind of nut can be used, and chopped prunes instead of raisins will also enhance what is a mixture between a savoury and sweet dish.

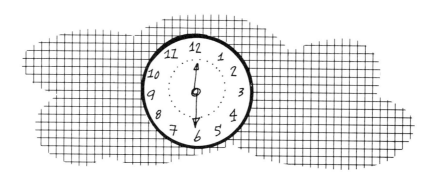

Not-just-stodge pizza

One of the bargain family meals of all time, for which the base is the only bit for which a recipe is needed. After that, you can pile on whatever you have available from the long list of toppings that suit pizzas. The one rule is that dry ingredients don't suit pizza baking: so cooked beans, raw cauliflower or cooked rice, for instance, will go crispy and hard, not tasty.

(Serves 4 — about 350 calories each, depending on toppings.)

Imperial (Metric)	American
4 oz (100g) wholemeal plain flour	1 cupful wholemeal plain flour
1 heaped teaspoonful baking powder	1 heaped teaspoonful baking powder
A good pinch of sea salt	A good pinch of sea salt
2 tablespoonsful vegetable margarine or cold-pressed olive oil	2 tablespoonsful + 2 teaspoonsful vegetable or cold-pressed olive oil
Some milk for mixing dough	Some milk for mixing dough
4 oz (100g) onion, chopped	1 cupful onion, chopped
6 tomatoes or 1 × 14 oz (400g) tin	3 cupsful tomatoes
½ teaspoonful oregano	½ teaspoonful oregano
1 rounded teaspoonful mixed dried herbs	1 rounded teaspoonful mixed dried herbs
4 oz (100g) Cheddar or Mozarella cheese	1 cupful Cheddar or Mozarella cheese

Toppings: your choice of one or many of these: tinned sardines or tuna, olives, sliced mushrooms, sweetcorn, cooked courgettes (zucchini), slices of green or red pepper, chopped or halved walnuts (English walnuts), pine nuts and sunflower seeds, artichoke hearts.

Heat oven to maximum temperature. Sieve flour with baking powder and salt. Fork in half the margarine or oil, and enough milk to make a soft dough. Roll or pat out as thinly as possible, to cover baking tin with side rims at least ¾ in. deep. Bake for 10 minutes. Meanwhile, turn onion gently in remaining fat, adding mushrooms if using. After 5 minutes, add tomatoes, half the herbs, and fish or sweetcorn if using. Break up fish and tomatoes with a fork.

Remove base from oven, spread with tomato mixture followed by whatever other toppings you are using except olives or walnuts. Grate the cheese evenly over the top, sprinkle with herbs and olives or walnuts if using. Return to hot oven for 10 minutes until cheese has melted.

Vegetable crumble

Like stir-fried vegetables, a dish you can make twenty times, each time made different by the mix of vegetables that you have handy or which are in season.

(Serves 4 — about 295 calories each using peas, 285 using mushrooms.)

Imperial (Metric)	**American**
2 medium onions	2 medium onions
2 carrots	2 carrots
2 sticks celery	2 sticks celery
¼ cabbage	¼ cabbage
¼ cauliflower	¼ cauliflower
Large wedge of swede or turnip	Large wedge of rutabaga or turnip
2 parsnips	2 parsnips
4 oz (100g) mushrooms or peas	2 cupsful mushrooms or 1 cupful peas
1 teaspoonful cornflour	1 teaspoonful cornstarch
1 tablespoonful soya/tamari sauce	1 tablespoonful soya/tamari sauce

For crumble

1½ oz (45g) soft margarine	Scant ¼ cupful soft margarine
4 oz (100g) wholemeal flour or ground brown rice	1 cupful wholemeal flour or ground brown rice
1 oz (25g) ground hazelnuts	¼ cupful ground hazelnuts

Heat oven to 400°F/200°C (Gas Mark 6). Place 1 in. water in saucepan and bring to the boil. Thinly slice vegetables into boiling water adding the hardest and therefore longest-cooking vegetables first. Cover and boil for 8 minutes. Drain, reserving cooking liquid. Place vegetables in casserole. Stir enough cold water into the cornflour (cornstarch) to make a smooth paste. Gradually stir in stock from cooked vegetables and place over heat, stirring until thickened. Add soya/tamari sauce and pour over vegetables in casserole. To make topping, rub fat into flour until mixture resembles breadcrumbs in consistency and stir in nuts. Pour over vegetables and bake for 20 minutes.

Nut slice

(Serves 4-6 — about 410 or 275 calories each.)

Imperial (Metric)	**American**
1 large onion	1 large onion
4 oz (100g) mixed ground nuts	1 cupful mixed ground nuts
1 oz (25g) soya flour	¼ cupful soya flour
1½ oz (45g) sesame seeds	4 tablespoonsful sesame seeds
1½ oz (45g) sunflower seeds	4 tablespoonsful sunflower seeds
1 teaspoonful mixed dried herbs	1 teaspoonful mixed dried herbs
½ teaspoonful sea salt or herb salt	½ teaspoonful sea salt or herb salt
2 eggs	2 eggs
4 oz (100g) mushrooms	2 cupsful mushrooms
1 oz (25g) toasted wholemeal breadcrumbs	¼ cupful toasted wholemeal breadcrumbs
1 oz (25g) vegetable oil or soft vegetable margarine	¼ cupful vegetable oil or soft vegetable margarine
¼ pint (150ml) stock	½ cupful stock

Heat oven to 375°F/190°C (Gas Mark 5). Grate the onion into a large mixing bowl. Add nuts, flour, seeds, herbs and salt. Mix in eggs. Chop mushrooms and add. Turn mixture into a greased 9 in. pie dish, sprinkle with breadcrumbs and remaining fat. The mixture will look quite dry. Pour over the stock. Bake for 25 minutes. Serve hot or cold with green salad.

Mrs F. Spitzer, Leigh-on-Sea, Essex

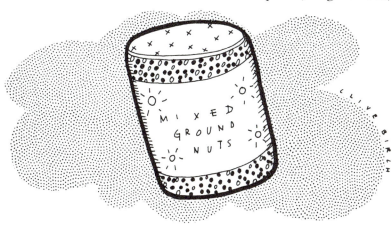

Black-eye beans

Black-eye beans — which look very like haricot beans, with a marked black 'eye' in the centre — are the only pulse apart from split peas and lentils that need no soaking. What's more, they cook to tenderness in just 35 minutes — a bit of a cheat for this section, but permissible, we feel, to bring these useful items to your attention.

To cook, simply rinse a cupful of beans in a sieve under a running tap to wash, place in pan with 2 of the same cupsful of water, bring to the boil, and simmer covered for 35 minutes. 4 oz (100g, ½ cupful) of dry beans will cook to 8 oz (225g, 1 cupful) of cooked beans — a good portion for two. Their flavour is not very strong, so you may want to 'spice them up'. Once cooked, you can use your beans to make some of these:

1. While beans are cooking, make a ratatouille-style vegetable mixture to combine with them. Turn a sliced onion (and a clove of garlic, if liked) in a very little oil until softening, then add sliced courgettes (zucchini), thinly sliced aubergines (egg plants), green pepper and 4 or 5 tomatoes. Cook gently until tender, which will take about the same time as the beans. If using fresh tomatoes (you could use a 14 oz/400g tin), add 1 large tablespoonful of tomato *purée* (paste) near the end of cooking. Season with basil if liked, and a little sea salt or soya/tamari sauce.

2. You can make a more English-style vegetable mixture in the same way, but adding thick matchsticks of carrot, parsnip, swede (rutabaga), potato, marrow or celery to the basic onion and 14 oz or 1 medium tin of tomatoes. In this case, flavour with the thoroughly British herbs of thyme and sage. If you add 1 tablespoonful each of cider vinegar and raw cane sugar, you will have a near-baked-beans flavour.

3. You can make a delicious bean soup by softening a finely chopped onion in a little oil, then adding your large cupful of raw beans and water, plus 3 cupsful of stock. Simmer for 35 minutes, then liquidize with 1 teaspoonful of tarragon and lemon juice to taste (about 2 tablespoonsful) for a 'main course' protein soup. Sprinkle with chopped parsley.

Note: these beans contain about 80 calories per ounce (when raw — less when cooked).

Lentil soup

A big contribution to the protein of a meal, lentil soup is a true convenience food, and a favourite with most people. Make it a complete meal with wholemeal rolls and a salad. Or pour it into a vacuum flask for a warming away-meal.

(Serves 3-4 — about 155 or 116 calories each.)

Imperial (Metric)	American
1 onion	1 onion
1 carrot	1 carrot
2 teaspoonsful vegetable oil or vegetable margarine	2 teaspoonsful vegetable oil or vegetable margarine
4 oz (100g) split red lentils	⅓ cupful split red lentils
1 bay leaf	1 bay leaf
1¼ pint (750ml) stock	3 cupsful stock
Sea salt and black pepper	Sea salt and black pepper
Chopped parsley	Chopped parsley

Chop onion and carrot finely (or grate for speed). Soften in the fat for 5 minutes in saucepan. Meanwhile, rinse lentils in sieve under tap, picking out any black bits. Add to onions with bay leaf and stock. Boil then simmer covered for 15-20 minutes, when lentils will be tender. Add seasoning and chopped parsley. If liked, sieve or liquidize. For a packed meal, only boil for 10 minutes at home, then transfer to vacuum flask, where cooking will finish perfectly.

Gnocchi ★

An Italian dish that can be eaten instead of potatoes — or as a main course, with one of the vegetables that naturally complements it — such as broccoli, cauliflower or crinkly ½ in. wide ribbons of Savoy cabbage, all cooked only to crunchy stage.

Traditionally, the mixture is left to cool before baking, but the cook-in-a-hurry will still find this quicker version satisfactory.

(Serves 4 — about 375 calories each.)

Imperial (Metric)	American
1 ½ (850ml) skim milk	3 ¾ cupsful skim milk
6 oz (180g) farina (potato flour) or wholewheat semolina	⅔ cupful farina (potato flour) or wholewheat semolina
½ teaspoonful sea salt	½ teaspoonful sea salt
1 small onion, grated	1 small onion, grated
2 eggs	2 eggs
4 oz (100g) grated Cheddar cheese	1 cupful grated Cheddar cheese

Pre-heat oven to 350°F/180°C (Gas Mark 4). Boil water for base of double boiler, or saucepan in which another saucepan you own will sit stably. Meanwhile, mix milk, farina or semolina, salt and onion in top pan. Stir over the simmering water for about 10 minutes.

Remove from heat, beat in one egg at a time. Then stir in three-quarters of the cheese. Spread mixture on a lightly oiled flat dish so that it is no more than 1 in. deep. Cover with remaining cheese and bake for 20 minutes. Remove from oven, brown quickly under the grill.

Flora flan

Soft margarine speeds pastry making, especially if you use the Flora method where the water is mixed in with the fat. Of course this would work with any other margarine that is high-in-polyunsaturates.

To fit a 30-minute deadline, flans should be baked blind, while you prepare the filling. (See also Thinking Ahead section.)

(Serves 4 — about 335 calories each.)

For pastry

Imperial (Metric)	**American**
2 oz (50g) polyunsaturated margarine	¼ cupful polyunsaturated margarine
1 tablespoonful (15ml) water	1 tablespoonful water
4 oz (100g) wholemeal plain flour	1 cupful wholemeal plain flour

Filling 1

1 oz (25g) polyunsaturated margarine	1 ½ tablespoonsful polyunsaturated margarine
1 onion, sliced	1 onion, sliced
1 oz (25g) wholemeal plain flour	¼ cupful wholemeal plain flour
7 fl oz (200ml) skim milk	¾ cupful skim milk
3 in. (7.5cm) length of cucumber, sliced	3 in. (7.5cm) length of cucumber, sliced
3 tomatoes, sliced	3 tomatoes, sliced
½ teaspoonful oregano	½ teaspoonful oregano
Sea salt and black pepper	Sea salt and black pepper
3 oz (75g) Edam cheese, grated	¾ cupful Edam cheese, grated
1 sliced tomato to garnish	1 sliced tomato to garnish
Parsley to garnish	Parsley to garnish

Pastry Case: Pre-heat oven to 400°F/200°C (Gas Mark 6). Place margarine, water and about a third of the flour in a bowl and cream with a fork for about 30 seconds until well mixed. Stir in remaining flour to form a firm dough.

Lightly flour work surface or pastry board and roll out pastry to fit 7 in. flan case. Lightly oil flan case and carefully lift pastry into case. Trim edges and place piece of greaseproof paper inside pastry case. Fill with old beans (baking beans) and bake for 10 minutes. Take from oven and remove paper and beans, storing beans for future use. The 'baked blind' flan case is now ready for filling.

Filling 1: Melt margarine and *sauté* sliced onion until soft. Add flour and cook over low heat for 1 minute. Remove pan from heat, gradually work in milk to make a smooth mixture. Return to heat, stirring continuously until mixture thickens. Simmer for 1-2 minutes. Add cucumber and tomato slices, cook for another 3-5 minutes. Add herbs and seasoning, and about two-thirds of the cheese.

Remove flan case from oven, fill with the mixture. Sprinkle with remaining cheese and return to oven until it melts. Decorate with tomato and parsley before serving.

Filling 2: As above, but add 6 oz (180g, 3 cupsful) of mushrooms, in place of the cucumber and tomato. Slice them into pan as you *sauté* the onion.

Cheese bake ✔

A blender recipe, to put together in a minute or two.

(Serves 4-6 — about 250 or 167 calories each.)

Imperial (Metric)
2 oz (50g) mature Cheddar cheese
3 oz (75g) wholemeal plain flour
1 egg
8 fl oz (250ml) semi-skim or skim
   milk
½ teaspoonful sea salt
Good pinch of black pepper
½ teaspoonful oregano
2 oz (50g) walnut pieces

American
½ cupful mature Cheddar cheese
¾ cupful wholemeal plain flour
1 egg
1 cupful semi-skim or skim milk
½ teaspoonful sea salt
Good pinch of black pepper
½ teaspoonful oregano
½ cupful English walnut pieces

Pre-heat oven to 425°F/220°C (Gas Mark 7). Cut piece of cheese in half and grate. Put half with all the other ingredients except nuts in the blender. Mix quickly. Grease a pie dish, stir nuts into blender goblet and pour mixture into dish. Bake for 25 minutes. Grate on remaining cheese and cook a further 2 minutes.

Stuffed mushrooms ★

(Serves 4 — about 130 calories each.)

Imperial (Metric)
12 large flat mushrooms
A little vegetable oil for brushing
   mushrooms
2 shallots or spring onions
1 teaspoonful butter or soft
   margarine
1 tablespoonful wholemeal plain
   flour
6 tablespoonsful single or sour
   cream
3 tablespoonsful finely chopped
   parsley
2 tablespoonsful grated Parmesan
   cheese

American
12 large flat mushrooms
A little vegetable oil for brushing
   mushrooms
2 shallots or scallions
1 teaspoonful butter or soft
   margarine
1 heaped teaspoonful wholemeal
   plain flour
8 tablespoonsful single or sour
   cream
4 tablespoonsful finely chopped
   parsley
2 rounded tablespoonsful grated
   Parmesan cheese

Pre-heat oven to 375°F/190°C (Gas Mark 5). Remove stalks from mushrooms. Use pastry brush to coat caps sparsely with oil, set hollow-side-up in shallow lightly greased ovenproof dish.

Chop onions or shallots, cook in the butter or margarine over a low heat, adding finely chopped mushroom stalks as you prepare them. Reduce heat, stir in the flour for 1 minute. Remove from heat, stir in cream until smooth, heat very very gently until thickening. Stir in the parsley, divide mixture between mushroom caps, top each with a little of the cheese and bake for 15 minutes or until tender.

Watercress and mushroom soufflé ✓

Sounds good, tastes good, looks good — and is really easy. Must be eaten immediately.

(Serves 4 — about 270 calories each.)

Imperial (Metric)	American
2 oz (50g) soft margarine	¼ cupful soft margarine
4 oz (100g) mushrooms	2 cupsful mushrooms
1 clove garlic (optional)	1 clove garlic (optional)
2 oz (50g) wholemeal plain flour	½ cupful wholemeal plain flour
½ pint (300ml) skim milk	1¼ cupsful skim milk
1 bunch watercress	1 bunch watercress
½ teaspoonful sea salt	½ teaspoonful sea salt
2 teaspoonsful mild mustard	2 teaspoonsful mild mustard
Good pinch of nutmeg	Good pinch of nutmeg
4 eggs	4 eggs

Pre-heat oven to 375°F/190°C (Gas Mark 5). Melt margarine in largish saucepan, stir in sliced mushrooms and crushed garlic if using. Turn over gentle heat, then cover for 2 minutes. Stir in flour over gentlest heat for 1 minute. Remove pan from stove. Gradually work in the milk smoothly, return pan to stove and heat gently, stirring until mixture is thick and leaves the sides of the pan as you stir. Remove from heat again. Add finely chopped watercress, salt, mustard and nutmeg, then thoroughly beat in each egg yolk separately. Beat egg whites stiff, fold in gently. Brush 4 small casseroles with oil lightly. Divide mixture between them, bake for 20-25 minutes until risen and beginning to brown, using top shelf of oven.

Mushroom bake

(Serves 4 — about 215 calories each.)

Imperial (Metric)	**American**
1 onion	1 onion
1 teaspoonful vegetable oil or soft vegetable margarine	1 teaspoonful vegetable oil or soft vegetable margarine
8 oz (225g) mushrooms	4 cupsful mushrooms
1 teaspoonful yeast extract	1 teaspoonful yeast extract
6 oz (175g) cottage cheese	¾ cupful cottage cheese
8 oz (225g) fresh wholemeal breadcrumbs	4¼ cupsful fresh wholemeal breadcrumbs
1 large teaspoonful dried mixed herbs *or*	1 large teaspoonful dried mixed herbs *or*
1 tablespoonful fresh herbs	1 heaped tablespoonful fresh herbs
Sea salt and black pepper	Sea salt and black pepper
1 oz (25g) Cheddar cheese, grated	¼ cupful Cheddar cheese, grated

Heat oven to 375°F/190°C (Gas Mark 5). Peel onion and grate coarsely into a frying pan brushed with the fat. *Sauté* for a few minutes. Meanwhile, in a small saucepan, turn chopped mushrooms in a few spoonfuls of water into which you have stirred the yeast extract.

Mix onions with cottage cheese, breadcrumbs, herbs and seasoning. Press half this mixture into lightly oiled ovenproof dish, top with mushrooms, and any liquid with them, then remaining mixture and grated cheese. Bake for about 20 minutes, until cheese is browned.

Crusty aubergine

The same technique can be used on large courgettes (zucchini).

(Serves 4 — about 240 calories each.)

Imperial (Metric)
1 ½ lb (675g) aubergines (2 fairly large)
2 medium eggs
2 oz (50g) dry wholemeal breadcrumbs
1 oz (25g) Parmesan cheese, freshly grated
1 tablespoonful chopped parsley
¼ teaspoonful sea salt
Pinch of black pepper
1 oz (25g) wholemeal plain flour
3 tablespoonsful vegetable oil or soft margarine

American
2 medium-to-large eggplants
2 medium eggs
½ cupful dry wholemeal breadcrumbs
¼ cupful Parmesan cheese, freshly grated
1 tablespoonful chopped parsley
¼ teaspoonful sea salt
Pinch of black pepper
3 tablespoonsful wholemeal plain flour
¼ cupful vegetable oil or soft margarine

Pre-heat oven to 400°F/200°C (Gas Mark 6). Wash aubergine (eggplants), and cut into slices ½ in. thick. The peel can stay on — if it turns out to be too chewy, it can always be cut off by the eater. Beat eggs slightly. Mix breadcrumbs, cheese, parsley, salt and pepper on a sheet of greaseproof paper. Dip slices in flour, then in egg, then coat thoroughly in crumb mixture. Shake off excess. Use the oil or margarine to grease fairly generously one very large or two small baking sheets. Arrange aubergine (eggplant) slices on tins. Bake uncovered for 25 minutes, turning at half-time.

Desserts

Instant cheesecake ✓

Once you've tried the flavour of this super-quick pudding, you may wonder why people go to all the extra trouble of conventional cheesecake recipes: this is delicious.

5 minutes.

(Serves 4 — about 230 calories each, or 154 if divided between 6.)

Imperial (Metric)
4 small oranges or peaches
1 lb (450g) low-fat soft cheese*
1 oz (25g) honey or molasses
Several drops natural vanilla
    flavouring
1 oz (25g) sunflower seeds or
    chopped nuts

American
4 small oranges or peaches
2 cupsful low-fat soft cheese*
1 tablespoonful honey or molasses
Several drops natural vanilla
    flavouring
¼ cupful sunflower seeds or
    chopped nuts

Chop fruit and mix with cheese, honey and vanilla. Heap into four sundae dishes. If using sunflower seeds, toast for 2 minutes in dry frying pan (skillet) over low heat, then sprinkle seeds or nuts on top of cheese mixture.

Optional extras: add a handful of raisins; extra fresh fruit in season; biscuit crumbs (wholemeal) or wheatgerm to give extra body.

    *If using cottage cheese, sieve to make it smoother.

Date delight

5 minutes.

(Serves 4 — about 148 calories each or 186 if using bananas.)

Imperial (Metric)
4 apples, bananas or small oranges
Juice of ½ lemon (not needed if
    using oranges)
Handful of dates, chopped
2 tablespoonsful coconut (dried,
    unsweetened)
½ pint (300ml) natural low-fat
    yogurt
Cinnamon to garnish

American
4 apples, bananas or small oranges
Juice of ½ lemon (not needed if
    using oranges)
Handful of dates, chopped
3 tablespoonsful coconut (dried,
    unsweetened)
1 ¼ cupsful natural low-fat yogurt
Cinnamon to garnish

Wash apples, peel other fruit. Chop oranges finely, grate apple or mash bananas. Sprinkle apple or banana with lemon (or orange) juice immediately to prevent browning. Add other ingredients, serve in sundae dishes sprinkled with cinnamon.

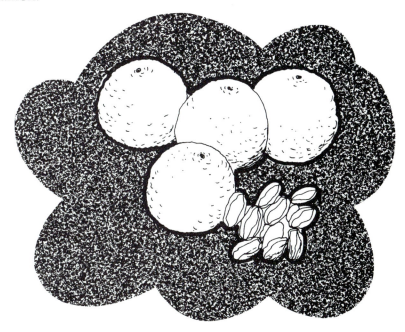

Raisin and apple Scotch pancakes

A quick dessert, to serve with hot stewed rhubarb or to eat with fingers in front of the television, these little drop scones are just as useful for unexpected tea-time guests, breakfast or packed meals.

5 minutes.

(Makes about 16 × 2 in. diameter pancakes — 55 calories each.)

Imperial (Metric)	American
4 oz (100g) wholemeal plain flour	1 cupful wholemeal plain flour
1 teaspoonful mixed spice	1 teaspoonful mixed spice
2 teaspoonsful baking powder	2 teaspoonsful baking powder
Pinch of sea salt	Pinch of sea salt
1 large egg	1 large egg
Just over ¼ pint (150-200ml) semi-skim or skim milk	Just over ¾ cupful semi-skim or skim milk
Vegetable oil for cooking + 2 teaspoonsful	Vegetable oil for cooking + 2 teaspoonsful
1 tablespoonful clear honey	1 large tablespoonful clear honey
2 oz (50g) raisins	⅓ cupful raisins
1 good-sized eating apple	1 good-sized eating apple

Sieve flour with spice, baking powder and salt, returning any bran left in sieve to the mixing bowl. Add the egg and gradually work in the milk to make a smooth, thick batter. Add 2 teaspoonsful of oil, honey, raisins and finally the apple cut into small chunks. Brush a thick-based frying pan with oil and heat thoroughly. Drop spoonsful of the mixture, allowing a little room for spreading. Cook over a low-to-medium heat for about 45 seconds, until the top side shows bubbles. Turn pancakes to brown on other side. Stack to keep warm on hot shallow dish.

Instead of serving with butter, use cottage cheese or raw sugar jam — or try them just by themselves.

Pouring custard ✓

The non-custard powder way. Many people are so surprised at how nice it tastes, they eat it as dessert all on its own.

8 minutes.

(Serves 4 — about 98 calories each, or 85 using skim milk.)

Imperial (Metric)	American
½ pint (300ml) semi-skim or skim milk	1 ¼ cupsful semi-skim or skim milk
1 tablespoonsful honey or Demerara sugar	1 tablespoonful honey or Demerara sugar
Few drops of natural vanilla essence or 1 vanilla pod, split	Few drops of natural vanilla essence or 1 vanilla pod, split
2 eggs	2 eggs
Ground nutmeg	Ground nutmeg

If you are using skim milk powder, use 3 good tablespoonsful to ½ pint of water. This gives the custard a creamier taste. However, fresh semi-skim milk is preferable. Bring milk, sugar or honey and vanilla pod to the boil in a pan. Meanwhile, beat the eggs in a jug. When milk is at scalding point, pour on to the eggs, whisking as you pour. Take out vanilla pod if using.

Add vanilla essence if using. Return custard to pan, and reheat gradually, stirring constantly. The custard will thicken suddenly, when you should quickly remove from the heat. If the custard gets too hot and starts to curdle, return immediately to jug and whisk (or liquidize).

A grating of nutmeg enhances the flavour of custard.

Variations: if you are making custard for trifle, you may want to use a few tablespoonsful less milk, to achieve a thicker consistency.

Oat and honey grapefruit

If available, use pink grapefruit — they are sweeter and the colour is lovely. 8 minutes.

(Serves 4 — about 74 calories each.)

Imperial (Metric)	American
2 tablespoonsful rolled oats	2 rounded tablespoonsful rolled oats
2 tablespoonsful honey	2 generous tablespoonsful honey
2 large grapefruit	2 large grapefruit
Ground cinnamon	Ground cinnamon

Heat grill. Mix the oats and honey in a pan over low heat. Halve the grapefruit, and separate segments. Place halves on lightly greased grill pan, and divide oat mixture between them, spreading evenly over tops. Grill for about 5 minutes, on medium heat. Sprinkle with cinnamon and serve.

Orange pancakes

The wholefood version of *crêpes suzettes* — and one of the easiest quick puddings. This basic pancake recipe can be used for many sweet and savoury dishes. Pancakes can be made in advance or frozen. To do so, let each pancake cook separately on a rack, then stack and wrap in polythene for storage. Reheat from fridge or freezer on plate covered with foil or tin dish, sitting over pan of simmering water.
    10 minutes — makes 12 × 6 in. pancakes.

(Serves 4-6 — about 55 calories per pancake; 90 with sauce.)

Imperial (Metric)	**American**
Pinch of sea salt	Pinch of sea salt
4 oz (100g) plain wholemeal flour	1 cupful plain wholemeal flour
1 egg	1 egg
¼ pint (150ml) milk	1 cupful + 2 tablespoonsful milk
¼ pint (150ml) water	1 cupful + 2 tablespoonsful water
1 tablespoonful olive oil	1 tablespoonful olive oil

For orange sauce

1 large or 2 small oranges	1 large or 2 small oranges
1 oz (25g) butter or soft margarine	¼ cupful butter or soft margarine
2 tablespoonsful (50g) clear honey	2 tablespoonsful clear honey
1 tablespoonful Curacao,	1 tablespoonful Curacao,
Cointreau or Drambuie	Cointreau or Drambuie
(optional)	(optional)

If you have a liquidizer, put all the batter ingredients in and blend for 15-20 seconds. Otherwise, in a large jug add salt to flour, add egg and half of the milk. Mix, then add rest of milk and water and finally oil, beating in. Boil a saucepan of water, and simmer with a dinner-plate on top. Brush thick-based frying pan/skillet (cast iron is ideal) with oil, heat well. From liquidizer goblet or jug, pour the equivalent of three tablespoonsful of batter into one side of pan, while tipping it that way with other hand. Swirl batter round pan to cover as thinly as possible. Quickly pour any excess batter back into jug or goblet. Cook over medium heat for about 1 minute, until edges begin to lift. Turn pancake, cook otherside for 1 minute. Tip on to heated plate.
    If first pancake was too thick, thin batter with a little more milk. Continue making pancakes, re-oiling pan only if your *crêpes* have started to stick.

Sauce

Finely grate peel and squeeze juice from orange(s). Put butter or margarine in pan after making *crêpes*, add all ingredients except liqueur if using. Heat gently and stir until sauce begins to bubble. Fold pancakes in half, and then half again, to make 'petticoat tails'. Lay in pan with orange sauce to heat for a few minutes, turning to coat. If using liqueur, add now, and when spirit has warmed, set alight. This will burn off the alcohol, but leave the flavour.

The average frying pan will only take about 4 or 5 pancakes at a time, so warm in sauce in batches, allowing two per dessert portion, and transferring to warm serving dish.

Other sweet pancakes fillings:

1. Traditional lemon juice, teamed with honey, for each person to add themselves at table.
2. As each pancake is made, spread with apple or soft fruit *purée* (sauce) (such as gooseberries, dried or fresh apricots, blackcurrants) and make a layered pile on your heated plate. Finish with a layer of fruit. To serve, cut into wedges like a cake. You will need at least 1 lb (450g) and preferably 1 ½ lb (700g) of fruit to make a generous filling. If you use all 12 pancakes, the result will serve 6 people.
3. Fill with fruit, as in no. 2, with the addition of a few flaked almonds which have been lightly toasted, in each layer. When pile is complete, beat 1 egg white with 1 tablespoonful of raw cane sugar until very stiff. Sprinkle on top of pile, with a few more almond flakes, and brown under grill for a few minutes.
4. Pancakes can also be rolled or stacked with: sliced peaches, flavoured with cinnamon; stewed rhubarb flavoured with mixed spice.

Joanna Pope

Gooseberry and wheatgerm dessert

Gooseberries go particularly well with wheatgerm. You can use *puréed* rhubarb, apple or blackcurrants instead. For a good thick *purée* (sauce), use only a little of the cooking water. Do not sweeten.
  10 minutes.

(Serves 4 — about 200 calories each.)

Imperial (Metric)
3 tablespoonsful (25g) wheatgerm
Juice of 2 oranges
1 lb (450g) *puréed* cooked
  gooseberries
4 tablespoonsful (40g) walnut
  pieces
A large orange, cut in segments
Grated rind of ½ the orange
10 oz (275g) natural low-fat yogurt
2 tablespoonsful (20g) slivered
  almonds
4 teaspoonsful (35g) clear honey

American
4 tablespoonsful wheatgerm
Juice of 2 oranges
3 cupsful gooseberry sauce
4 tablespoonsful English walnut
  pieces
A large orange, cut in segments
Grated rind of ½ the orange
1 ¼ cupsful low-fat yogurt
2 tablespoonsful + 2 teaspoonsful
  slivered almonds
4 teaspoonsful clear honey

Mix wheatgerm with orange juice, then add fruit *purée* (sauce), walnuts, orange segments and rind. Pile into sundae glasses, top with the yogurt, almond slivers and a teaspoonful of clear honey per glass.

Mrs Pat Michell, Cadishead, Manchester

Banana mousse

Cheaper, loose bananas will do very well for this recipe.
  10 minutes.

(Serves 4 — about 125 calories each.)

Imperial (Metric)	American
2-3 ripe bananas	2-3 ripe bananas
2-3 tablespoonsful single cream	3 tablespoonsful single cream
2 teaspoonsful honey or Barbados sugar	2 teaspoonsful honey or Barbados sugar
¼ pint (150ml) natural low-fat yogurt	½ cupful + 1 large tablespoonful natural low-fat yogurt
2 egg whites	2 egg whites
Cinnamon to garnish	Cinnamon to garnish

Place bananas, cream, sugar or honey in liquidizer goblet with the yogurt. Blend. Beat egg whites stiff and fold in. Divide into four glasses for serving. Sprinkle top with cinnamon if wished.

Mrs J. Adamson, Otford, Kent

Grilled bananas

8 minutes.

(Serves 4 — about 160 calories each.)

Imperial (Metric)	American
4 firm ripe bananas	4 firm ripe bananas
Rind and juice of a large orange	Rind and juice of a large orange
Pinch each of ground nutmeg, cinnamon and cardamom	Pinch each of ground nutmeg, cinnamon and cardamom
2 tablespoonsful honey or Barbados sugar	2½ tablespoonsful honey or Barbados sugar
2 tablespoonsful flaked almonds	2 tablespoonsful + 2 teaspoonsful flaked almonds

Pre-heat a grill and brush baking tray thinly with butter, margarine or vegetable oil. Place lengthways-split bananas halves on tray. Prick with fork 4 or 5 times. Mix juice, rind and spices in a cup, pour evenly over bananas. Sprinkle with sugar. Grill for 3-4 minutes, sprinkle with almonds and grill for a minute or two more until they are golden.

Sesame cheese balls

Like mini-cheesecakes, these can be eaten in the fingers as a dessert to go with something like grapes or coffee (decaffeinated!). They're also good child-tempters.

10 minutes.

(Makes 12 — about 45 calories each.)

Imperial (Metric)	**American**
1 teaspoonful grated lemon or orange rind	1 teaspoonful grated lemon or orange rind
2 oz (50g) slab dates	⅓ cupful slab dates
1 oz (25g) raisins or sultanas	¼ cupful raisins or golden seedless raisins
2 teaspoonsful bran	2 teaspoonsful bran
A few drops natural vanilla essence	A few drops natural vanilla essence
½ teaspoonful mixed spice	½ teaspoonful mixed spice
4 oz (100g) soft medium- or low-fat cheese*	½ cupful soft medium- or low-fat cheese*
1-2 tablespoonsful sesame seeds	1 ½ -2 tablespoonsful sesame seeds

Scrub orange or lemon thoroughly under hot water to remove any wax coating. Grate finely into bowl. Chop dates and raisins or sultanas finely, mix with bran which helps separate pieces. Blend in vanilla, spice and cheese. Roll into lozenge shapes between palms, and dip into sesame seeds to coat. Store chilled.

   *Must be a fairly dry variety — if not, drain through muslin.

Hot spiced fruit salad

You need a wide-mouthed vacuum flask for this recipe. Set it going when you start to prepare your quick meal, and it will be perfectly ready to eat by pudding time, served hot from the flask into dishes.

30 minutes.

(Serves 4 — about 125 calories each.)

Imperial (Metric)
8 oz (225g) dried 'fruit salad' — or your blend of dried apricots, peaches, nectarines, figs, apple rings, prunes, raisins, sultanas or currants
½ teaspoonful each ground cinnamon and nutmeg
1 lemon

American
2 packed cupsful 'fruit salad' — or your blend of dried apricots, peaches, nectarines, figs, apple rings, prunes, raisins, golden seedless raisins or currants
½ teaspoonful each ground cinnamon and nutmeg
1 lemon

Bring the fruit to the boil in enough water to cover. Simmer for 1 minute, drain and throw water away. Repeat the process with fresh water, pour some into flask to warm it. Then return to pan, reboil and tip fruit into flask with enough water to cover by 1 ½ in. Add spices and 3 slices of lemon. Close until wanted.

Variations: unsyruped figs are delicious cooked like this, eaten hot or cold.

Rhubarb crumble

Basic, and none-the-worse for that, rhubarb crumble is one of the best desserts, and speedier than most crumbles because rhubarb cooks so fast. The same recipe can be used with many other fruits.

30 minutes.

(Serves 4 — about 263 calories each.)

Imperial (Metric)	American
1 ½ lb (700g) fresh rhubarb	1 ½ pounds fresh rhubarb
1 oz (25g) sultanas	¼ cupful golden seedless raisins
4 tablespoonsful water	5 tablespoonsful water
1 sprig sweet cicely, if available	1 sprig sweet cicely, if available
2 oz (50g) Demerara or Muscovado sugar, or honey	⅓ cupful Demerara or Muscovado sugar, or honey

For topping

3 oz (75g) wholemeal plain flour	¾ cupful wholemeal plain flour
1 tablespoonful skim milk powder	1 heaping tablespoonful skim milk powder
1 oz (25g) butter or soft margarine	1 tablespoonful butter or soft margarine
1 oz (25g) any raw cane sugar	2 tablespoonsful any raw cane sugar

Pre-heat oven to 400°F/200°C (Gas Mark 6). Chop rhubarb in 1 in. lengths, and place in saucepan with the sultanas (golden seedless raisins), water and sweet cicely. This herb mysteriously takes some of the sour taste of fruit away — reducing the need for sweetening. Simmer for about 3 minutes, remove from heat. Layer rhubarb and drizzles of the honey or sugar in oven-proof dish. To make topping place flour and skim milk powder in mixing bowl and rub in fat. Stir in sugar and spread over rhubarb, cook for 25 minutes.

Note: for many kinds of fruit, you would need only 1 lb (450g) to serve four, and less sweetening. Rhubarb happens to 'cook down' in volume more than most, and to be sourer.

Hunza apricots

Quite different from other dried apircots in both looks and flavour, Hunza apricots look like unpromising grey, hard, ¾ in. diameter, wrinkled bullets when you buy them. The dull colour is because they haven't had their tint preserved with sulphur dioxide, as all yellow apricots have. These apricots are a staple food in Hunza, the North Indian kingdom which has long been famous for the health of its population. When cooked, however, preferably in a wide-mouthed vacuum flask. Hunza apricots turn into delicious little morsels with a distinctive taste. They are so sweet naturally, you need not add any extra sweetener.

   30 minutes' soaking.

(Serves 4 — about 104 calories each.)

Imperial (Metric)
8 oz (225g) Hunza apricots
A little grated lemon rind if liked

American
2 packed cupsful Hunza apricots
A little grated lemon rind if liked

Pick apricots over carefully, rejecting any that have signs of insect damage. Place in a pan, cover with water and bring to the boil. Simmer for 1 minute, drain and throw away water. Recover with fresh water, boil again. Pour some of the liquid into vacuum flask, if using, to warm it. Return to pan, boil and transfer all contents with lemon rind to warmed flask. Close for 30 minutes. If not using a flask, simmer covered for 30 minutes.

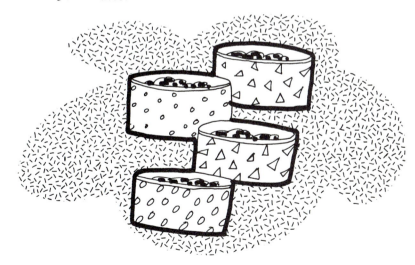

Baked apples

An apple called Howgate Wonder is our favourite for these — use sweeter apples, so you'll need less added sweetening. By the way, if you have a pressure cooker, these take just 3 minutes! For other cooks, avoid enormous apples if speed matters.

35 minutes.

(Serves 4 — about 80 calories each.)

Imperial (Metric)
4 large apples, about 6-7 oz
   (180-200g) each
1 teaspoonful mixed spice
½ teaspoonful cinnamon
2 oz (50g) mixed dried fruit
4 teaspoonsful honey
¼ pint (150ml) water

American
4 large apples, about 6-7 oz each
1 teaspoonful mixed spice
½ teaspoonful cinnamon
⅓ cupful mixed dried fruit
4 teaspoonsful honey
½ cupful water

Pre-heat oven to 400°F/200°C (Gas Mark 6). Wash apples, and place in oven-proof dish. With a sharp knife, slit the skin in a circle halfway down the fruit. Core, making quite large cavities. Mix the spice, cinnamon and dried fruit, and stuff into the core spaces. Drizzle 1 teaspoonful of honey over each apple, pour the water round the base of the apples. Bake for about 30 minutes.

Note: for the sake of speed, this recipe uses a slightly higher temperature than normally suggested. The result may be that your apples 'explode' and collapse. However, the slit round the skin helps avoid this; and they will still taste just as good.

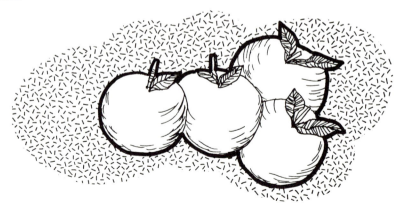

Bread pudding

Eat hot as a pudding, then cold as a cake or ideal lunch-box item.
35 minutes.

(Makes 6 hefty chunks — about 210 calories each.)

Imperial (Metric)

8 oz (225g) wholemeal bread or stale cake (or a mixture)
4 oz (100g) mixed dried vine fruit
1 oz (25g) margarine or butter
1 tablespoonful mixed spice
Good pinch of nutmeg and sea salt
2 oz (50g) honey, maple syrup or black treacle
1 egg

American

2 cupsful wholemeal bread or stale cake (or a mixture)
¾ cupful mixed dried vine fruit
¼ cupful margarine or butter
1 rounded tablespoonful mixed spice
Good pinch of nutmeg and sea salt
2 good tablespoonsful honey, maple syrup or molasses
1 egg

Pre-heat oven to 400°F/200°C (Gas Mark 6). Place the bread in a large sieve and run under the cold tap (the sieve drains the bread naturally, so you don't have any problems with it dissolving or getting too wet). When thoroughly soaked, press bread down to remove excess water. Make sure it crumbles easily in your hand. Place in bowl, add dried fruit, butter or margarine, spice, nutmeg, salt, honey or treacle and the egg. Mix thoroughly.

Transfer to a shallow, lightly greased baking dish and smooth the top. Sprinkle with more ground nutmeg and bake for 30 minutes, or until set.

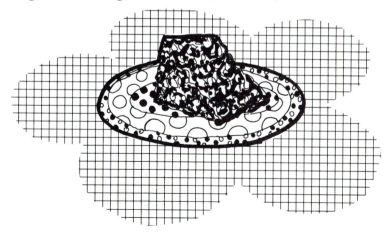

Millet egg pudding

The nearest thing to a rice pudding for cooks in a hurry. Millet's pale gold colour is a bonus for this really successful dish.

40 minutes.

(Serves 4 — about 285 calories each, or 225 using skim milk.)

Imperial (Metric)
2 oz (50g) millet flakes
1 ¼ pints (750ml) milk, skim if possible
3 eggs, beaten
Strip of lemon rind
2 oz (50g) Demerara or other raw cane sugar
Few drops natural vanilla essence

American
1 scant cupful millet flakes
3 cupsful milk, skim if possible
3 eggs, beaten
Strip of lemon
⅓ cupful Demerara or other raw cane sugar
Few drops natural vanilla essence

Pre-heat oven to 350°F/180°C (Gas Mark 4). Cook the millet flakes in the milk for a few minutes until thick. Stir in eggs, lemon rind, sugar and vanilla. Pour into a greased oven-proof dish and bake for 25 minutes, or until set.

Variations: use honey or molasses instead of sugar, as half the sweetening. Add a handful of chopped dried fruit to the recipe and you will need less sweetening of any kind.

Carol Hunter, H.H. Cookbook

Baking

Sesame bars

Spicy and easy to make, these are much lower in fat than the sesame snacks you'll find in shops.
   30 minutes.

(Makes 10 — about 68 calories each.)

Imperial (Metric)	American
1 egg	1 egg
1 ½ oz (45g) Muscovado sugar or honey	3 tablespoonsful Muscovado sugar or honey
1 ½ tablespoonsful butter or soft margarine	1 ½ tablespoonsful butter or soft margarine
1 oz (25g) wholemeal plain flour	¼ cupful wholemeal plain flour
Pinch of sea salt	Pinch of sea salt
Pinch of bicarbonate of soda	Pinch of baking soda
½ teaspoonful ground cinnamon	½ teaspoonful ground cinnamon
¼ teaspoonful ground nutmeg	¼ teaspoonful ground nutmeg
¼ teaspoonful allspice	¼ teaspoonful allspice
1 oz (25g) toasted sesame seeds	¼ cupful toasted sesame seeds

Heat oven to 350°F/180°C (Gas Mark 4). Beat the egg, slowly add the sugar. Stir in the melted fat. Then sieve in the flour, salt, soda, and spices. Grease an 8 in. baking tin extremely thoroughly. Sprinkle half the sesame seeds on base, spoon on mixture. Bake for 5 minutes. Sprinkle on remaining seeds, bake for further 20 minutes. Cut into fingers while warm and leave to cool in tin.

Soda bread

The quickest loaf bread — you can turn it out in 40 minutes.
40 minutes.

(About 67 calories per ounce, or slice.)

Imperial (Metric)

1 lb (450g) wholemeal plain flour
½ teaspoonful sea salt
1 teaspoonful bicarbonate of soda
2 teaspoonsful cream of tartar
1 oz (25g) vegetable oil or soft margarine
½ pint (300ml) skim milk, or a mixture of milk and water*

American

4 cupsful wholemeal plain flour
½ teaspoonful sea salt
1 teaspoonful baking soda
2 teaspoonsful cream of tartar
¼ cupful vegetable oil or soft vegetable margarine
1 ¼ cupsful skim milk, or a mixture of milk and water*

Pre-heat oven to 450°F/230°C (Gas Mark 8). Sieve flour, salt, soda and cream, of tartar together. Return most of bran in sieve to mixing bowl. Rub in fat or mix in with fork if using oil. Add enough liquid (the exact amount will depend on the flour you use) to make a soft dough.

Grease a fairly large baking tray. Turn dough onto baking tin, and knead quickly just to smooth out big cracks. Flatten with hand to about 1 ½ in. (4 cm) deep circle. Score deeply with knife. Brush top with milk, sprinkle with retained bran. Bake for 30-35 minutes.

Variations: sprinkle top of loaf with sesame seeds after brushing with milk. A spoonful or two of toasted sesame seeds added to the dough also adds an interesting flavour. Cool loaf on rack.

*Sour milk is excellent.

Christmas tree biscuits ★

It's well worth collecting a variety of cutters to give your biscuits an interesting and professional look. While this dough can of course be cut into other shapes, it makes beautiful, crisp-edged Christmas trees, with the split almonds suggesting extra branches.

20 minutes.

Imperial (Metric)	American
4 oz (100 g) butter	½ cupful butter
4 oz (100 g) light Muscovado sugar	¾ cupful light Muscovado sugar
1 small egg, beaten	1 small egg, beaten
8 oz (225 g) wholemeal plain flour	2 cupfuls wholemeal plain flour
1 teaspoonful baking powder	1 teaspoonful baking powder
4 oz (100 g) chopped mixed nuts	1 cupful chopped mixed nuts
Split almonds and walnut halves for decoration	Split almonds and English walnut halves for decoration

Pre-heat oven to 350°F/180°C (Gas Mark 4). Cream together the butter and sugar until pale and creamy. Beat in the egg with 1 tablespoonful of the flour. Mix in the remaining flour with the baking powder and chopped nuts to give a firm dough. Knead dough on a lightly floured surface, adding a little more flour it is is too sticky to roll out. Roll out ¼ in. thick. Stamp out biscuits, and place on lightly greased baking sheet. Press the split almonds on the edge of each tree 'branch', and if liked, half a walnut at the base to represent the tree trunk. Bake for 15 minutes until lightly browned.

Gingerbread queens

Good to have in reserve — a quick batch of these is easily made and they keep well in an air-tight tin. Adults enjoy them as much as children do.
    20 minutes.

(Makes 16 × 7 in. tall — about 162 calories each.)

Imperial (Metric)	American
12 oz (325g) wholemeal plain flour	3 cupfuls wholemeal plain flour
4 level teaspoonsful baking powder	4 level teaspoonsful baking powder
2 level teaspoonsful dry ginger	2 teaspoonsful dry ginger
4 oz (100g) soft vegetable margarine	½ cupful soft vegetable margarine
4 oz (100g) Demerara sugar	¾ cupful Demerara sugar
4 tablespoonsful molasses	5 tablespoonsful molasses
1 egg, beaten	1 egg, beaten

Pre-heat oven to 375°F/190°C (Gas Mark 5). Grease baking sheets. Sieve flour, baking powder and ginger into bowl, rub in margarine. Stir in sugar. Warm molasses and add with beaten egg to form a soft dough. Knead gently to smooth out cracks, roll ¼ in. thick (1cm). Cut with a gingerbread queen or gingerbread man cutter. Cool thoroughly before storing.

Raisin and apple muffins

A nice change for breakfast — especially if you've run out of bread — or for tea — for which you could add an ounce or two of honey or raw cane sugar if wished. 20-25 minutes.

(Makes 12 — about 70 calories per muffin, or 62 without sweetening.)

Imperial (Metric)	American
4 oz (100g) wholemeal plain flour	1 cupful wholemeal plain flour
2 rounded teaspoonsful baking powder	2 rounded teaspoonsful baking powder
1½ teaspoonsful mixed spice	1½ teaspoonsful mixed spice
Good pinch of sea salt	Good pinch of sea salt
1 large egg	1 large egg
¼ (150ml) pint skim milk	½ cupful skim milk
1 teaspoonful vegetable oil	1 teaspoonful vegetable oil
1 oz (25g) Demerara sugar/honey (optional)	¼ cupful Demerara sugar/honey (optional)
½ large apple, grated	½ large apple, grated
1 small carrot, grated finely	1 small carrot, grated finely
2 oz (50g) sultanas or raisins	⅓ cupful golden seedless raisins or raisins

Pre-heat oven to 400°F/200°C (Gas Mark 6). Sieve together the flour, baking powder, spice and salt. Beat egg, milk and oil and sugar/honey if using. Add to dry ingredients, stir in apple, carrot and sultanas/raisins quickly. Grease lightly 12 patty tins or use paper bun cases. Fill two-thirds full, bake for 15-20 minutes until springy.

For lighter muffins, retain any bran left in sieve after sifting flour, and sprinkle on top of muffin mixture in tins before baking.

The fruit loaf

A moist, tasty fruit loaf that needs no added fat, and gives the choice of a moderate amount of raw cane sugar, or honey instead. Include some chopped dried apricots, prunes or citrus peel in the fruit for best flavour.
1 hour 5 minutes.

(Makes 10 good slices — about 1550 calories using sugar, 1390 using honey, for whole loaf.)

Imperial (Metric)	American
8 oz (225g) mixed dried fruit	1½ cupfuls mixed dried fruit
3 oz (75g) Demerara sugar or 2 oz (50g) honey	½ cupful sugar or 2 tablespoonsful honey
6 tablespoonsful fruit juice, unsweetened	Scant ½ cupful fruit juice, unsweetened
5½ oz wholemeal pain flour	1¼ cupfuls wholemeal plain flour
3 level teaspoonsful baking powder	3 level teaspoonsful baking powder
½ teaspoonful mixed spice	½ teaspoonful mixed spice
Good pinch ground nutmeg	Good pinch ground nutmeg
1 large egg	1 large egg

Pre-heat oven to 325°F/170°C (Gas Mark 3). Mix dried fruit with sugar/honey and fruit juice. Sieve together the flour, baking powder and spices. Beat egg, and add to fruit mixture. Then add flour mixture. Mix well, bake in a well greased 1 lb loaf tin for 50-60 minutes, or until top is springy.

Apple and cheese loaf

A moist loaf that doesn't taste very apple-y, so is savoury rather than sweet. Its real appeal is when toasted — delicious, without needing spreading. Will only keep 2-3 days, because of apple.
45 minutes.

(Makes about 12 good slices — about 1250 calories for whole loaf.)

Imperial (Metric)	American
8 oz (225g) wholemeal plain flour	2 cupsful wholemeal plain flour
½ teaspoonful bicarbonate of soda	½ teaspoonful baking soda
½ teaspoonful sea salt	½ teaspoonful sea salt
½ teaspoonful mustard powder	½ teaspoonful mustard powder
½ teaspoonful baking powder	½ teaspoonful baking powder
4 oz (100g) grated strong-flavoured Cheddar cheese	1 cupful grated strong-flavoured Cheddar cheese
6 oz (175g) grated apple	1 packed cupful grated apple

Pre-heat oven to 400°F/200°C (Gas Mark 6). Sift flour, soda, salt, mustard and baking powder. Reserve most of the bran left in sieve. Mix in cheese and apple, then add enough extra liquid (water, milk) to make a stiff dough. Grease a loaf tin, and coat sides and base with most of reserved bran. Place dough in tin, sprinkle top with remaining bran. Bake for 30-40 minutes.

Apricot chew

A nice change from flapjacks, these are a cross between a flapjack and fruit bar. Although we have given weights, you can use the US cup measures for simplicity. 40 minutes.

(About 2045 calories for the batch.)

Imperial (Metric)	American
3 oz (75g) dried apricots	¾ cupful dried apricots
2 oz (50g) pumpkin seeds or nuts	½ cupful pumpkin seeds or nuts
4 oz (100g) wholemeal plain flour	1 cupful wholemeal plain flour
3 oz (75g) rolled oats	1 cupful rolled oats
1 small cupful bran	1 cupful bran
1 teaspoonful cinnamon	1 teaspoonful cinnamon
1 teaspoonful allspice	1 teaspoonful allspice
10 oz (280g) honey	1 cupful honey

Pre-heat oven to 350°F/180°C (Gas Mark 4). Chop or mince apricots and pumpkin seeds, and place in bowl with flour, oats, bran and spices. Gently heat honey, add to dry ingredients. Mix and press into lightly oiled tin, about 12 in. × 8 in. (30cm × 20cm). Bake for 25-30 minutes. Cut into slices while warm, removing from tin when cool.

J. Cairnes, Devizes, Wilts.

Gateau sponge

50 minutes.

(Makes 10 good slices — about 2370 calories, plus 570 for topping, for whole cake.)

Imperial (Metric)	American
5 oz (140g) wholemeal plain flour	1¼ cupsful wholemeal plain flour
1 oz (25g) cornflour	3 tablespoonsful cornstarch
2 level teaspoonsful baking powder	2 teaspoonsful baking powder
¼ teaspoonful sea salt	¼ teaspoonful sea salt
5 oz (140g) Demerara sugar	1 cupful Demerara sugar
2 eggs	2 eggs
3 fl oz (125ml) + 1 tablespoonful vegetable oil	½ cupful vegetable oil
Rind and juice of 1 large lemon	Rind and juice of 1 large lemon

Pre-heat oven to 350°F/180°C (Gas Mark 4). Oil and line and oil again two 7 in. sandwich tins. Sift the dry ingredients, adding sugar last. Retain any bran left in sieve. Beat egg yolks with oil and 3 fl oz (100ml) of cold water (US ½ cupful minus 1 tablespoonful). Beat into dry ingredients to form a smooth batter. Mix in lemon juice and rind. Whisk egg whites stiff but not dry. Fold in and divide between the two tins.

Bake for about 40 minutes, until centres are springy. Allow to cool in tins for a minute or two, before turning out on to rack.

Variation: For a 'chocolate' cake, add 1 oz (25g, ¼ cupful) of carob flour to flour when sieving, and a few drops of natural almond essence to oil mixture. Increase added water by 2 teaspoonsful.

Fillings and Toppings

1. Blend by hand, adding yogurt last: 8 oz smooth low-fat cheese (225g, 1 US cupful), 1 chopped orange, 2 tablespoonsful natural yogurt and enough thick honey to sweeten to your taste. Use for 3 layers of filling, reserving ¼ for topping.
2. Simmer and then *purée* 8 oz dried apricots (225g, 1 ¾ US cupsful) in the minimum of the cooking water so the *purée* (sauce) is very thick. If too thin, add ground almonds to thicken. Use for 3 layers of filling, reserving ¼ for topping.
3. *Topping*: Reserve some of either filling to make topping. If using apricots, mix remaining *purée* (sauce) with low-fat soft cheese, vanilla essence and a little honey for topping. Sprinkle cake with flaked or chopped nuts, or garnish with fresh fruit.
4. *To eat immediately*: Delicious but quickly soggy, so requiring quick consumption is a filling of *purée* soft fruit, such as raspberries (uncooked) or lightly cooked gooseberries, blackberries or blackcurrants. These can be creamed with low-fat, smooth soft cheese. The *purée* (sauce) must be made as thick (dry) as possible.

Brandy snaps ✓

Who would have thought of brandy snaps as a convenient food? They are —
as well as being a good store-cupboard item, if you have a really air-tight tin.
Use them to dress up fruit or iced desserts as well as in packed lunches or for tea.
20 minutes.

(Makes 10 — about 100 calories each.)

Imperial (Metric)	American
2 oz (50g) butter or soft vegetable margarine	¼ cupful butter or soft vegetable margarine
2 oz (50g) Demerara sugar	⅓ cupful Demerara sugar
2 oz (50g) black treacle or honey	2 teaspoonsful molasses or honey
2 oz (50g) wholemeal plain flour	½ cupful wholemeal plain flour
1 teaspoonful ground ginger	1 teaspoonful ground ginger

Pre-heat oven to 325°F/170°C (Gas Mark 3). Heat butter, sugar and treacle
(molasses) or honey gently until dissolved. Place pan in refrigerator while you
sift flour with ginger. Add to mixture, stir well. Grease two baking sheets. Place
teaspoonsful of the mixture at least 4 in. apart, cook for 8 minutes. Remove tins
from oven and after about 2 minutes, detach one brandy snap at a time, using
a sharp knife. Turn over so underside is outward as you roll it round the handle
of a wooden spoon. Work quickly as brandy snaps become brittle as they cool.
Roll tighter than you think — they tend to unwind on the cooling rack. If snaps
become brittle, return tray to oven for a minute to re-soften.

Fruit Loaf (page 92), Brandy Snaps (page 96),
Christmas Tree Biscuits (page 90). ▶

Johnny cake

One of the foods on which the American pioneers built the West! The most important element for success is unrefined cornmeal which has not been kept too long: it should be sweet, not rancidly bitter. Johnny cake is neither sweet nor savoury, but something in between, to eat instead of bread, hot with soups, savouries or stewed fruit, or with honey for tea. It's fairly solid — don't expect fairy-cake lightness.

30 minutes.

(Makes 16 squares — about 82 calories each.)

Imperial (Metric)	American
4 oz (100g) yellow maizemeal	¾ cupful cornmeal
4 oz (100g) wholemeal plain flour	1 cupful wholemal plain flour
½ teaspoonful sea salt	½ teaspoonful sea salt
2 ½ teaspoonsful baking powder	2 ½ teaspoonsful baking powder
2 tablespoonsful Demerara sugar*	2 rounded tablespoonsful Demerara sugar
8 fl oz (250ml) milk, preferably skim	1 cupful milk, preferably skim
1 egg, well beaten	1 egg, well beaten
2 tablespoonsful oil or melted margarine	2 tablespoonsful oil or melted margarine

Pre-heat oven to 400°F/200°C (Gas Mark 6). Sift maizemeal (cornmeal), flour salt and baking powder together, then add the sugar. Add milk, egg and finally fat. Beat well, pour into well greased 8 in. square baking tin, and bake for 25-30 minutes. Cut into squares.

*You can omit the sugar for a less authentic corncake that goes better for English tastes as a bread replacement or with savouries.

Thinking Ahead

Frozen plum pudding ★

If you don't like Christmas pudding, here's your answer, in a recipe that originated in Australia, where Christmas falls in midsummer. But use this recipe for special desserts all year round too.

15 minutes plus freezing time.

(Serves 8 — about 400 calories each.)

Imperial (Metric)	American
2 teaspoonsful gelatine	2 teaspoonsful gelatin
½ pint (300ml) water	1¼ cupsful water
3 eggs	3 eggs
4 oz (100g) raw cane sugar	¾ cupful raw cane sugar
1½ cupsful* (250g) mixed dried fruit	1¾ cupsful mixed dried fruit
½ cupful mixed chopped nuts	⅔ cupful mixed chopped nuts
Juice and grated rind of 1 orange	Juice and grated rind of 1 orange
1 cupful wholemeal breadcrumbs	1¼ cupsful wholemeal breadcrumbs
1 cupful double cream	1¼ cupsful heavy cream

Soak the gelatine in a little of the water in a heatproof bowl. Stand the bowl in a pan of hot water and stir until dissolved. Allow to cool while separating the eggs and beating the yolks slightly. Simmer sugar and water for 5 minutes then pour over yolks stirring as you do so. Return to heat and cook very gently until mixture thickens. Do not allow to boil. As soon as mixture thickens remove from heat and cool. When mixture is nearly cold gradually stir in the gelatine. Stiffly beat egg whites and fold in. Stir in the mixed fruit, nuts, juice and rind of orange, and the breadcrumbs. Beat cream until very thick, fold in. Pour mixture into a large savarin or other fancy mould and freeze until wanted.

Remove from freezer to refrigerator about 40 minutes before you plan to eat this. Decorate at Christmas with holly, otherwise with mint leaves.

*use a cup that will hold 10 fl oz (300ml) of water.

Pashka

A much richer version of this recipe is the traditional Russian Easter dish: packed with cream, butter and eggs, it emphatically shows that Lent is over. It's often made there in a special mould with the letters XB standing for 'Christ has risen'. The distinctive shape of whatever mould you use is important to this dish: you could use a new flower pot or a sieve, both of which have the advantage or helping drain off the whey.

It's a super-easy recipe to make in advance.

20 minutes plus draining time.

(Serves 8-10 — about 300 or 240 calories each†.)

Imperial (Metric)	American
1 ½ lb (675g) soft, medium- or low-fat cheese	3 cupsful soft, medium- or low-fat cheese
2 oz (50g) walnut, almond or hazelnut pieces	½ cupful English walnut, almond or hazelnut pieces
1 large egg	1 large egg
2 oz (50g) butter or soft margarine	¼ cupful butter or soft margarine
1 oz (25g) finely grated orange peel*	¼ cupful finely grated orange peel*
1 oz (25g) dried apricots, chopped	¼ cupful dried apricots, chopped
2 oz (50g) raisins	⅓ cupful raisins
2 oz (50g) currants	⅓ cupful currants
¼ teaspoonful natural vanilla essence	¼ teaspoonful natural vanilla essence
A few spoonfuls of honey	A few spoonfuls of honey
A few spoonfuls of natural yogurt or sour cream	A few spoonfuls of natural yogurt or sour cream

Optional: candied or crystallized fruit, eg. chopped fried chunks of pineapple, papaya, pear or orange. Split almonds to decorate.

The most important step is to ensure that the cheese is as dry as possible — and smooth. If you use cottage cheese, rub it through a sieve. Grate nuts coarsely or chop. Beat egg and mix with butter or margarine into some of the cheese to soften it. Then mix in all remaining ingredients, adding honey to taste at the end, and just enough yogurt or sour cream to give a workable texture.

Line the dish to be used with muslin or any coarse-textured thin white cloth. Leave enough material to fold over top of the container. Pack mixture into mould, cover with material and place a plate and then a weight (such as a tin) on top. Stand in fridge or cold place for 12 hours.

To serve, unmould removing cloth gingerly: you want to keep the surface perfect, marked with the 'weave' pattern of the cloth. Pashka can be decorated with toasted whole almonds, or an Easter chick in season.

*The traditional recipe uses candied peel, which isn't very healthy as it is very sugary. Finely grated orange peel, coupled with chopped dried apricots, makes a good substitute in colour and flavour terms.

†Allowing for medium-fat curd cheese, 2 oz honey (50g, 2 large tablespoonsful) and up to 4 oz yogurt (100g, ½ cupful) or 1½ oz (45g, 3 tablespoonsful) sour cream.

Rollmop herrings ✓

These are ready to take out of your store cupboard for an instant meal after one week.

(Makes enough for 6 fish — about 234 calories per 100 grams of raw fish.)

Imperial (Metric)	American
6 herrings, fresh	6 herrings, fresh
2 oz (50g) sea salt	¼ cupful sea salt
1 pint (600ml) water	2½ cupsful water
1 large onion, chopped fine	1 large onion, chopped fine
1 tablespoonful pickling spice	1 heaped tablespoonful pickling spice
1 tablespoonful peppercorns	1 rounded tablespoonful peppercorns
1 bay leaf	1 bay leaf
1 chilli pepper	1 chilli pepper
1 pint (600ml) malt vinegar	2½ cupsful malt vinegar

Clean, bone and fillet fish. Dissolve the salt in the water and soak fish overnight, skin side up. Next day, drain, rinse in fresh water and dry fish. Roll each one up with a little of the finely chopped onion in the middle, and pack tightly into a large jar with coated lid — uncoated insides of metal lids will quickly corrode with the vinegar.

Add pickling spices, peppercorns, bay leaf and chilli pepper and pour the vinegar over, to cover fish completely. Secure lid tightly.

Fish kebabs ✓

Could be made in 10 minutes, but tastes much better if the fish is marinated for
about an hour or so.

   At least 1 hour's soaking plus 10 minutes cooking.

(Serves 4 — about 220 calories each.)

Imperial (Metric)
1¼ lb (565g) chunky fish — coley
   will do well
1 large onion
16 mushrooms
8 mini (cherry) tomatoes, or 8
   chunks of green pepper
4 long skewers

For marinade

1 tablespoonful cold-pressed olive
   or other oil
2 tablespoonsful lemon juice
2 tablespoonsful dry white wine
1 clove garlic, crushed (optional)
1 teaspoonful ground cumin or
   coriander
Freshly ground black pepper
1 teaspoonful mustard

American
1¼ pounds chunky fish — coley
   will do well
1 large onion
16 mushrooms
8 mini (cherry) tomatoes, or 8
   chunks of green pepper
4 long skewers

1 tablespoonful cold-pressed olive
   or other oil
2 tablespoonsful + 2 teaspoonsful
   lemon juice
2 tablespoonsful + 2 teaspoonsful
   dry white wine
1 clove garlic, crushed (optional)
1 teaspoonful ground cumin or
   coriander
Freshly ground black pepper
1 teaspoonful mustard

Combine marinade ingredients in a bowl. Cut fish (skinned, if skin is thick) into
rough 1 in. chunks and onions into eighths, then immerse in marinade, stirring
well. Leave for at least 1 hour. Line grill pan with foil and heat grill well. Thread
skewers with pieces of fish, thin segments of onion, whole mushrooms and
tomatoes, or pepper. Place on grill pan, brush with remaining marinade. Grill
for 4 minutes, turn and rebrush. Serve with plain grain, such as bulgur wheat,
buckwheat or with a bed of spinach.

Beansprouts

A home-grown ingredient that will turn out very useful when you want a quick meal.

Using a sprouter or a wide-mouthed large glass jar, fill one third full with one of the following that you have rinsed well in a sieve under the tap: mung beans, aduki beans, alfalfa seeds, whole unpeeled lentils, chick peas (garbanzo beans) or whole (uncracked) wheat grain. With tiny alfalfa seeds, drain through cloth or very fine sieve. If using a sprouter, follow instructions for rinsing sprouts with water. If using a glass jar, cover the mouth with a j-cloth or muslin, held on with a rubber band. Twice a day, run the tap through the cloth to fill the jar two-thirds full, shake well and drain off the water by leaving the jar upside-down on draining board.

Depending on the warmth of the room and time of year, the seeds will start to sprout in 2-3 days. Wheat sprouts are one of the quickest; alfalfa slowest. Use most sprouts when the sprout is as long as the seed. Mung and alfalfa shoots, however, will get 1-2 in. (2½-5cm) long before mature.

Once grown, you can use your beansprouts as a salad ingredient; added at the last minute to stir-fry vegetable dishes (see Chinese Vegetables on page 29); to add to savoury flan fillings; or just as a nibble by themselves. You can keep fully grown sprouts in a covered container in the refrigerator for 3 or 4 days. Sprouts are rich in many vitamins and minerals, contain under 10 calories per ounce and are very economical to grow, especially in winter when salad stuff may be expensive or limited in variety. Although the Chinese beansprouts which are grown from mung beans are the most familiar to us, the others are just as easy to get to like. Alfalfa sprouts are a little like mustard and cress (and why not get back to that again?). Chick pea (garbanzo bean) sprouts are particularly nice mixed with cubes of cheese and cucumber in salad.

Note: Do not sprout kidney beans, red or white.

Tabbouleh

A 'main course' type of salad to serve with other salads, such as grated carrot-lemon juice-nuts; watercress-beetroot; sprouted wheat-cubed cheese, and wholemeal rolls as a meal.

     35 minutes.

(Serves 4 as part of meal as above — about 160 calories each.)

Imperial (Metric)	**American**
5 oz (140g) bulgur wheat	½ cupful bulgur wheat
2 oz (50g) parsley, fresh	Good bunch parsley, fresh
3 good sprigs of mint leaves	3 good sprigs of mint leaves
A few spring onions	A few scallions
1 clove of garlic, crushed	1 clove of garlic, crushed
1 tablespoonful cold-pressed olive oil	1 tablespoonful cold-pressed olive oil
Juice of 1 lemon	Juice of 1 lemon
Sea salt and black pepper to taste	Sea salt and black pepper to taste

Wash bulgur wheat in a sieve under the tap — and just leave it in the sieve, where it will swell remarkably without getting too wet. Meanwhile, chop parsley coarsely and mint leaves and onions more finely, crush garlic and combine all the ingredients except salt and pepper. When a grain of the wheat tastes tender (but springy) all the way through, press wheat down in sieve to remove any excess water and combine with remaining items. Add sea salt and pepper to taste. You may also like to add a little more lemon juice. Let salad stand for a few minutes before serving if possible. It will improve in flavour if kept in the 'fridge for up to 24 hours.

Sprouted Seeds, Rollmop Herrings (page 101), Apricot Spread (page 111), Flans for Filling (pages 114 and 115). ▶

Spicy red cabbage

A 'solid' kind of vegetable that can complete a main course if served with one of the dishes it particularly complements, such as buckwheat or rice dishes.
1½ hours.

(Serves 6 — about 78 calories each.)

Imperial (Metric)	American
1 small head of red cabbage	1 small head of red cabbage
2 onions	2 onions
1 tablespoonful vegetable oil or margarine	1 tablespoonful vegetable oil or margarine
1 large cooking apple	1 large cooking apple
½ oz (15g) Muscovado or Demerara sugar	1 tablespoonful Muscovado or Demerara sugar
Juice of 2 lemons	Juice of 2 lemons
1 tablespoonful cider vinegar	1 tablespoonful cider vinegar
1 teaspoonful sea salt	1 teaspoonful sea salt
2 cloves	2 cloves
6 peppercorns	6 peppercorns

Boil a large kettle of water. Meanwhile, shred the cabbage finely into a large heatproof container. Pour the boiling water over the cabbage to blanch it. Leave for 1 minute — drain. Don't worry about the nasty colour, it will be alright later! Cook the sliced onions gently in the oil or margarine for 5 minutes. Add the cabbage, chopped apples (unpeeled) and all other ingredients. Stir, cover and after bringing to the boil, simmer for about 1¼ hours. Remember to remove cloves and peppercorns (or at least warn the family) before serving. Check seasoning. This dish actually improves after a day or so's keeping.

Oranges in liqueur

Simple and elegant.
5 minutes preparation.

(Serves 4 — about 70 calories each.)

Imperial (Metric)
4 medium oranges
1 tablespoonful honey or raw cane
  sugar
2 tablespoonsful liqueur: orange-
  flavoured one like Cointreau, or
  cherry brandy with its red tint,
  are ideal

American
4 medium oranges
1 tablespoonful honey or raw cane
  sugar
2½ tablespoonsful liqueur: orange-
  flavoured ones like Cointreau, or
  cherry brandy with its red tint,
  are ideal

With a peeler, cut 8 strips of peel (avoiding pith) from oranges. Using a sharp knife, peel all the skin and pith from oranges on a cutting board. Place the whole oranges in a glass serving bowl (or in four individual bowls). Sprinkle with the sugar or honey, then with the liqueur, and the strips of orange peel which you've trimmed to 2 in. (5cm) long, very narrow ribbons.

Allow oranges to marinate for several hours, turning if possible occasionally.

Note: If you object to alcohol in food, heat the liqueur slightly, then put a match to it before pouring over oranges. The alcohol will burn off, leaving the flavour more or less intact.

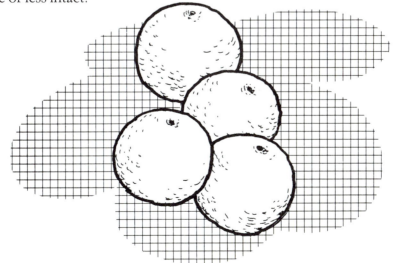

Kissel

This is very quick indeed to make, but needs some time to cool. You can make it with many different kinds of fruit, but black and redcurrants are the most traditional in Denmark, it's country of origin.

    5 minutes preparation.

(Serves 4 — about 82 calories each.)

Imperial (Metric)	American
1 lb (450g) soft fruit	1 pound soft fruit
¼ pint (150ml) water	½ cupful + 2 tablespoonful water
Honey to taste — about 2 oz (50g)	2 good tablespoonsful honey
1 tablespoonful cornflour	1 rounded tablespoonful cornstarch

Bring to the boil the fruit, water and honey. Simmer for only 2-3 minutes, then liquidize. Mix cornflour (cornstarch) with a little cold water to make a smooth paste. Add fruit to cornflour, return mixture to pan and cook for about 2 minutes, until smooth and clear. Cool and decorate with sprigs of currants or fruit leaves.

Fruit lollipops ✔

When you have a spare moment, fill lollipop moulds with your favourite fruit juice, or a mixture — for instance, pineapple and orange juice mixed half and half.

Hot Spiced Fruit Salad (page 83), Frozen Plum Pudding (page 99), Instant Cheesecake (page 74), Orange Sorbet (page 112). ▶

Little egg custards ✓

So easy to put together, but taking too long to cook to meet the 'fast meal' bill, these are more appealing in small pots. A favourite dessert for many people. 50 minutes plus cooking time.

(Serves 4-5 — 183 or 146 calories each.)

Imperial (Metric)	American
1 pint (600ml) semi-skimmed or skimmed milk	2½ cupsful semi-skimmed or skimmed milk
4 eggs	4 eggs
1 oz (25g) honey or Demerara sugar	2 tablespoonsful honey or Demerara sugar
Few drops of natural vanilla essence	Few drops of natural vanilla esence
Nutmeg to garnish	Nutmeg to garnish

Pre-heat oven to 325°F/170°C (Gas Mark 3). Boil a kettle of water. Meanwhile, heat milk to just scalding point. Whisk eggs lightly with the honey or sugar and vanilla. Pour hot milk on to egg mixture, beating as you go. Pour mixture to almost fill 4 or 5 ramekins or little bowls, set in roasting tin. Surround with an inch or two of the boiling water. Bake for 40-45 minutes, until custard is set. Serve in the bowls, with nutmeg grated on top, or turn out before grating nutmeg on.

Note: If using skim milk powder, make up stronger than usual — say, 2½ oz (60g, ¾ cupful) powder to 1 pint (600ml, 2½ cupful) of water, instead of usual 2 oz (50g, ⅔ cupful). Heat this kind of milk carefully and gradually — it tends to burn.

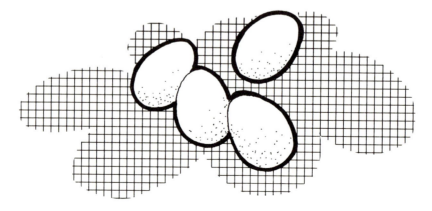

Apricot spread

A multi-purpose spread to use as a flan filling, a cake filling, on toast instead of surgary jam, or whipped with yogurt and egg whites as a fluffy dessert. It also forms a good ice cream base. It will keep for about 10 days in the refrigerator if covered and in a clean jar.

(Makes one 10 oz/250g pot — about 30 calories per oz/1 tablespoonful, or 295 for potful with honey, 21 per oz without.)

Imperial (Metric)	**American**
4 oz (100g) dried apricots	1 cupful dried apricots
1 tablespoonful honey (optional)	1 tablespoonful + 1 teaspoonful honey (optional)

Bring apricots to boil in water — simmer for a few minutes. This is to help boil off sulphur dioxide, and is also a good way of washing them. Now throw away water. Cover again with a fresh water and simmer for about 25 minutes or until tender. This can be done very easily by bringing to the boil and pouring into a wide-mouthed vacuum flask.

Using the minimum of cooking water so as to keep result thick, *purée* soft apricots. Add honey. Return to stove until boiling. If too thin, simmer uncovered now to evaporate some liquid. Otherwise, transfer to jar rinsed well in boiling water. Cover.

Variation: you can add some orange rind to this recipe for a kind of apricot-orange flavour. Finely chopped walnuts (English walnuts) are another good blend of flavours: chop freshly to add at the end of cooking before potting.

Orange sorbet

A lovely dinner party dessert which can be made well in advance.
   20 minutes plus freezing time.

(Serves 4 — about 90 calories each.)

Imperial (Metric)
4 large oranges
Juice of ½ lemon
2 tablespoonsful thick honey
A little extra orange juice may be
   needed
2 egg whites

American
4 large oranges
Juice of ½ lemon
2 heaping tablespoonsful thick
   honey
A little extra orange juice may be
   needed
2 egg whites

Cut a flat slice from the top of each orange about quarter way down. Hollow
out oranges (a grapefruit knife is helpful). Liquidize flesh, add lemon juice and
honey. Make up to ¾ pint (425ml, 1½ cupsful) with extra orange juice if
necessary. freeze until mixture begins to set Beat well, fold in stiffly whisked
egg whites and fill into orange skins allowing room at the top for expansion.
Freeze it and leave to thaw for about 1 hour in 'fridge before serving. Serve with
'lids' or with a sprig of fresh mint on top.

Humus

If you follow our tip of cooking in batches, you may have a handy bowl of cooked chick peas (garbanzo beans) from time to time ready for this quick and delicious pâté-cum-dip.

Use it as a popular stater at a dinner party, in a communal dish which guests dip into with pieces of raw carrot, cucumber slices, thin wholemeal toast or strips of toasted wholemeal pitta bread or chapatti. Use it with cucumber and cress to stuff pitta breads, for neat-to-eat party or picnic fare. Use it to make a good topping for baked potatoes.

1 hour.

(Serves 4-5 as dinner 'starter' — about 180 or 145 calories each.)

Imperial (Metric)	American
4 oz (100g) chick peas	¾ cupful garbanzo beans
1 clove of garlic	1 clove of garlic
Handful of parsley	Handful of parsley
1 teaspoonful ground cumin	1 teaspoonful ground cumin
1 tablespoonful cold-pressed olive oil	1 tablespoonful cold-pressed olive oil
Sea salt and black pepper	Sea salt and black pepper
Juice of 1-2 lemons	Juice of 1-2 lemons
1-2 tablespoonsful tahini (sesame cream)*	1-2 tablespoonsful tahini (sesame cream)*
4 oz (100g) low-fat soft cheese	½ cup low-fat soft cheese

Either soak chick peas (garbanzo beans) overnight in cold water, or use the method on page 12. Change the water, just covering the chick peas (garbanzo beans), and bring to the boil. Cover and simmer for about 50 minutes until tender. (Batches vary — they may take as long as 1 ½ hours). Place chick peas (garbanzo beans) in liquidizer with the peeled clove of garlic, parsley, cumin, olive oil, a little sea salt and pepper, and the juice of 1 lemon. Add enough of the cooking liquid to enable liquidizer to work, and blend to a smooth, thick paste. Now add 1 tablespoonful of tahini and the soft cheese, and blend again. Taste for flavour, adding more lemon juice or tahini as wanted. The humus will actually improve with a day's keeping, and will keep for two or three days covered in the refrigerator.

*You can buy tahini or make it — recipe on page 46.

Flans for filling

Flan cases can be kept for future use for at least a week in an air-tight tin, or much longer in a freezer. So when you have time to make pastry, make up three or four cases, say two to freeze, two to keep for later that week.

Use these methods:
a. Conventional shortcrust pastry made with wholemeal plain flour, plus half its weight in butter, vegetable fat or margarine. Use a fraction more water than you would for white pastry, as the bran will soak up some.
    To ease rolling out, do so on a floured sheet of polythene or foil, which you can then invert with the pastry over dish to be lined, peeling off backing carefully. This avoids the pastry breaking. If you want lighter, shorter pastry, 1) add a teaspoonful of baking powder to each 8 oz (225g, 2 cupsful) of flour; 2) sieve flour before use, retaining the bran in the sieve. Then use the bran to 'flour' the rolling surface, and scatter any remainder over flan before cooking.
b. Use the speedy all-in-one method on page 69.
c. For a lower-fat pastry, use the quick and easy-to-handle hot water crust usually employed for raised pies. Sieve 8 oz (225g, 2 cupsful) wholemeal plain flour with ½ teaspoonful salt. Bring 3 fl oz water (90ml, scant ½ cupful) to the boil with 2 oz (50g, ¼ cupful) butter or solid vegetable fat. When boiling, pour quickly into the flour, and mix to form a smooth paste. Working as soon as it's cool enough to handle, pat or roll out to fit required surface. Use slightly thicker than shortcrust pastry — about ¼ in. (½ cm) thick. This makes enough for 2 medium flan cases.
    Pre-heat oven to 400°F/200°C (Gas Mark 6). Weight centre of flan cases to prevent rising with foil or greased paper covered with beans. Bake for 15 minutes, remove centre weight and bake for 5 minutes more. Cool thoroughly before storage.
    If a flan becomes a little soft in storage, replace in a hot oven for a few minutes before serving.

Savoury flans
1. Scramble eggs lightly, top with thinly sliced tomatoes.
2. Scramble eggs with shrimps, prawns or shreds of smoked salmon.
3. *Sauté* in the minimum of butter or oil 8 oz (225g, 4 cupsful) sliced mushrooms, stir in two or three large spoonsful of either sour cream or yogurt (after which you must not boil), and season with lots of white pepper, a little sea salt and a grating of nutmeg.
4. Fill with ratatouille, cooked fairly dry, top with grated cheese and brown under the grill.

5. Fill with flaked cooked fish, in white sauce made with the fish cooking liquid, and flavoured with parsley, capers or cheese. Garnish with parsley and lemon wedges.
6. Fill with lightly cooked vegetables, cover with ½ pint (300ml, 1 ¼ cupsful) sauce, made with cooking liquid and/or milk.
7. Fill with sliced boiled onions, cheese sauce made with onion cooking liquid, and grated cheese on top, grilled to melt.

Sweet flans

1. *Purée* 1 lb (450g) of cooked apples, plums, apricots or 1 ½ lb (675g) of rhubarb, using only part of cooking water, so result is thick. Sweeten to taste with honey. If using apples or rhubarb, add a good handful of sultanas (golden seedless raisins) or raisins.
2. Poach apple or pear halves carefully in a little water. avoiding breaking them. Drain and arrange carefully in flan case. Add 1 tablespoonful of the fruit cooking water to 4 oz (100g, ⅓ cupful) apricot or redcurrant jam with a good squeeze of lemon juice. Boil and stir, then simmer for a few minutes before brushing generously over fruit. You can also use a few slices of stem ginger, with a little of the syrup heated, to add to the apricot or redcurrant glaze.
3. Fill with home-made lemon curd. Top with a layer of unsweetened desiccated coconut, and brown under a low grill.
4. Fill with lemon curd or fruit *purée* (sauce), top with 2 egg whites beaten stiffly with 2 tablespoonsful Demerara sugar. Brown quickly under hot grill.

Useful Extras

Coconut balls

The quickest way to make these is with a mincer (on fine blade) or in a food processor.

10 minutes.

(About 1509 calories for batch.)

Imperial (Metric)	American
6 oz (175g) chopped dates	1 ¼ cupsful chopped dates
2 oz (50g) stoned raisins	⅓ cupful stoned raisins
1 oz (25g) chopped almonds	¼ cupful chopped almonds
1 oz (25g) chopped walnuts	¼ cupful chopped English walnuts
1 oz (25g) chopped cashews	¼ cupful chopped cashews
1 oz (25g) honey	1 tablespoonful honey
2 oz (50g) desiccated unsweetened coconut	⅔ cupful desiccated unsweetened coconut

If using a mincer, put everything but honey and coconut through. Mix fruit and nuts with honey. Shape into 1 in. balls, roll in desiccated coconut. If liked, put in small paper cases for neat storage and presentation.

Ms D. Zhuraw, London W1

Coconut Balls (page 116), Ginger Delight (page 122), Honey Ratafias (page 118), Mincemeat (page 118), Popcorn (page 119).➤

Honey ratafias

Useful for dressing up desserts — and a delicious little munch to serve with coffee, like a *petit four*.
  20 minutes.

(Makes 28 — 24 calories each.)

Imperial (Metric)
2 egg whites
3 oz (75g) ground almonds
4 level tablespoonsful honey
Rice paper sheets

American
2 egg whites
¾ cupful ground almonds
5 tablespoonsful honey
Rice paper sheets

Pre-heat oven to 400°F/200°C (Gas Mark 6). Beat egg white stiff, mix in almonds and honey. Place in teaspoonsful on rice paper, allowing a little room to spread. Bake for about 10 minutes until golden brown at 250°F/180°C (Gas Mark 4).

Mincemeat

Don't save mincemeat for Christmas. Keep some handy for stuffing baked apples; for filling flans (then top with quickly grilled mixture of 2 egg whites (whisked stiff) and 2 tablespoonsful of raw cane sugar beaten in); or for spicing up stewed rhubarb or pears.
  20 minutes.

(Makes 3 lbs — about 62 calories per ounce.)

Imperial (Metric)
8 oz (225g) eating apples
1 large orange
4 oz (100g) almonds
8 oz (225g) currants
8 oz (225g) raisins
8 oz (225g) sultanas
2-3 teaspoonsful mixed ground
    spice
½ teaspoonful ground nutmeg
Orange juice, unsweetened
2 tablespoonsful brandy

American
2 small apples
1 large orange
¾ cupful almonds
1⅔ cupsful currants
1½ cupsful raisins
1½ cupsful golden seedless raisins
2 teaspoonsful mixed ground spice
½ teaspoonful ground nutmeg
Orange juice, unsweetened
2 tablespoonsful brandy

Scrub apples and orange thoroughly with hot water. Using the coarsest blade of mince, mince first the almonds, then the dried fruit, then the orange, and finally the cored but unpeeled apples. Stir to prevent apple browning. Now add mixed spice and nutmeg. Taste and adjust spice. Add enough orange juice to moisten slightly, then brandy. Transfer mixture to clean, dry jars and store in cool place.

Note: because this mincemeat does not contain added sugar or fat, it will not keep so well as conventional types — although the brandy will help. It is doubly important to use very clean, preferably sterilized jars. If you don't have a cold larder, keep jars in the refrigerator. Aim to use within 6 weeks. If fermentation occurs, don't worry — when the mincemeat is cooked, it will taste as normal. But if mould occurs, throw mincemeat away.

Popcorn

A much underused food in Britain, popcorn makes a crunchy snack which is high in nutrition, and relatively low in calories.

3 minutes.

(About 130 calories per ounce cooked.)

Imperial (Metric)	American
½ oz (15g) oil — olive or corn	1 tablespoonful oil — olive or corn
2 oz (50g) popcorn	4 tablespoonsful popcorn

To make successful popcorn, you need a heavy-based saucepan with a tight-fitting lid.

Heat oil in pan over a medium heat, until it is very hot. (Olive and corn oil are preferable because they are less liable to burn.) Tip in popcorn, close lid tightly and shake pan over medium heat for a few seconds to coat kernels with oil. Now leave pan over very low heat. After a little while, you will hear the corn start to pop. Do not take the lid off the pan to see what is happening! Leave pan closed until you have not heard a 'pop' for about 15 seconds.

Tip popcorn into serving bowl. It can be eaten just as it is, or stir a spoonful of yeast extract into the corn while it is still hot in the cooking pan. A sparing amount of sea salt or honey are other options.

Dressings

No. 1. *Seafood* (total: 60 calories, serves 2)

Imperial (Metric)

2 large tablespoonsful tomato
  purée
1 large tablespoonful thick, low-fat
  yogurt
1 teaspoonful fresh lemon juice or
  cider vinegar
Freshly ground black pepper
1 teaspoonful Worcestershire
  sauce

American

3 tablespoonsful tomato paste
2 tablespoonsful thick, low-fat
  yogurt
1 teaspoonful fresh lemon juice or
  cider vinegar
Freshly ground black pepper
1 teaspoonful Worcestershire
  sauce

No. 2. *Non-mayonnaise* (blender recipe)
(total: 284 calories, serves 6)

Imperial (Metric)

3 tablespoonsful wine or cider
  vinegar
2 tablespoonsful sieved wholemeal
  plain flour
8 fl oz (240ml) boiling water
1 egg
1 teaspoonful Demerara sugar
1 teaspoonful mild mustard
3 tablespoonsful sour cream

American

4 tablespoonsful wine or cider
  vinegar
3 tablespoonsful sieved wholemeal
  plain flour
1 cupful boiling water
1 egg
1 teaspoonful Demerara sugar
1 teaspoonful mild mustard
Scant ½ cupful sour cream

Blend vinegar and flour smoothly in a saucepan, stir in the boiling water whisking over a low heat. Simmer for about 8 minutes. Transfer mixture to a blender and add the egg, sugar and mustard. When well mixed, stir in the sour cream gradually by hand until you have a smooth texture. Taste and adjust seasoning if wished. Store in a closed jar in refrigerator.

No. 3. *Blue cheese*
(total: 280 calories, serves 4)

Imperial (Metric)	**American**
5 fl oz (150ml) low-fat yogurt	1 cupful + 1 good tablespoonful
2 oz (50g) crumbled Danish Blue	low-fat yogurt
cheese*	½ cupful crumbled Danish Blue
2 teaspoonsful fresh lemon juice	cheese*
A pinch of dry mustard	2 teaspoonsful fresh lemon juice
Sea salt and black pepper to taste	A pinch of dry mustard
	Sea salt and black pepper to taste

Mix all ingredients, and adjust seasoning.
*101 calories per ounce, versus 131 per ounce for Stilton.

No. 4. *Non-French*
(total: 160 calories, serves 2-3)

Imperial (Metric)	**American**
1 tablespoonful mild vinegar, e.g.	1 tablespoonsful mild vinegar, e.g.
wine	wine
1 tablespoonful fresh lemon juice	1 tablespoonful fresh lemon juice
½ tablespoonful favourite oil	¾ tablespoonful favourite oil
A pinch of Demerara sugar *or* a dab	A pinch of Demerara sugar *or* a dab
of honey	of honey
½ teaspoonful mild French	½ teaspoonful mild French
mustard	mustard
Fresh chives or parsley, chopped	Fresh chives or parsley, chopped

Blend all the ingredients, adjust seasoning.

Ginger delight

A delicious after-dinner sweet (and ginger aids digestion), or a good alternative to biscuits to eat with a cup of something mid-afternoon. A box of these and the other 'sweeties' we suggest would make a popular gift.

15 minutes.

(Makes 8 — about 58 calories each.)

Imperial (Metric)	American
1 oz (25g) butter or soft vegetable margarine	¼ cupful butter or soft vegetable margarine
3 tablespoonsful freshly chopped nuts	3 heaped tablespoonful freshly chopped nuts
1 oz (25g) fresh ginger, grated from a 2 oz (50g) root	2 large tablespoonsful fresh ginger, grated from a 2 oz (50g) root
4 level tablespoonsful Demerara sugar	¼ cupful Demerara sugar
½ teaspoonful cinnamon	½ teaspoonful cinnamon

Grate ginger until fine and paste-like. Boil in a little water in a small, heavy-bottomed saucepan for a few minutes. Drain off all water, add butter and sugar and stir over a low flame until the mixture holds its shape. Remove from heat and stir in the cinnamon. The mixture is very soft. To make it easier to handle allow to cool completely before rolling into small balls and dipping in finely chopped nuts. Place in individual paper cases for storing and serving.

Ginger delight makes a very strong ginger-flavoured result — so make very small balls. Delicious if you like ginger, however.

J. Bonner, Aviemore, Sherwood Rd, Tideswell, Derbyshire

Packed Meal Choices That Save You Time

If you make packed meals regularly, it's worth having a good, roomy lunchbox, a small Thermos flask and plastic cutlery. Keep cottage cheese cartons and small plastic and paper bags for packing salads and small items in.

1. *Sandwiches* are still good meals if you use wholemeal bread, are mean with butter or margarine, and favour low-fat high-salad fillings — see page 31. If you make a lot of packed meals each week, you can save time by making up a whole sliced wholemeal loaf of sandwiches (without salad), and freezing packed in pairs. They thaw out between packing and midday quite satisfactorily.

    To complete a sandwich meal, pack with it something fresh — chunks of carrot, cucumber or celery are less squashable than tomatoes. Watercress, mustard and cress and alfalfa sprouts are all good extras.

2. A Thermos of a light soup — such as Courgette and Tarragon, page 36, or a more solid one — such as Cream of Mushroom or Lentil (pages 37 and 67) — sets the scene for a salad lunch, with mixed shredded vegetables packed into cottage cheese cartons. Include some cottage or other low-fat soft cheese, or grated hard cheese, to complete this meal with a wholemeal roll or crispbreads — and plastic fork and spoon.

3. Any of our recipes for Peanut Patties, Cheese and Oat Burgers, Sesame Patties or Fish Cakes makes a good packed lunch item: make a double batch for the week's packed meals ahead.

    Complete with salad, as above, and a piece of fresh fruit.

4. Whole-meal Muesli (see page 44) makes a good summer packed meal, made with generous amounts of fruit. Pack in cottage cheese carton with a chunk of Apricot Chew (page 94) or some biscuits and cheese to follow.

5. Pack a mixed salad, with a hard-boiled egg, or peanuts in it, to be followed by a chunk of Bread Pudding (page 87), remembering that the latter provides protein as well as energy.

6. Other recipes worth considering with packed meals in mind: baked apples taste almost better when cold; wholemeal pitta bread or chapattis, filled with Tjatjiki cucumber-and-yogurt or with humus — both providing enough protein, from yogurt and chick peas (garbanzo beans) respectively, plus the bread's protein; smoked fish pâté in a small cheese carton, teamed with a wholemeal roll; crisp Christmas tree biscuits; Gingerbread Queens; slices of fruit loaf; Instant Cheesecake, to follow a salad or to eat with Brandy Snaps and fresh fruit; a Thermos of Hot Spiced Fruit Salad (page 83) with a carton of plain yogurt to stir into it when you eat it, and a couple of Apple and Raisin Pancakes; wedges of cold Spanish omelette to go with a salad; home-made popcorn (in a big bag), to add fun to a sandwich meal.

Menus For Entertaining

Dinner Parties

If you can plan ahead, even if you have little time to prepare just beforehand, you can offer guests menus like these:

Smoked Mackerel Pâté
with Oatcakes

* * *

Watercress *Soufflés*
with extra watercress
and sliced carrots

* * *

Orange Sorbet

Tjatjiki — cucumber and yogurt
dip, with wholewheat rolls

* * *

Fish Kebabs with
Spicy Red Cabbage and
spinach

* * *

Kissel

Humus (chick pea/garbanzo bean
pâté) with dips of raw
vegetables and wholemeal
Melba toast

* * *

Vegetable Crumble
with plain buckwheat
and a dish of grated
cheese to sprinkle over

* * *

Hot Spiced Fruit Salad
with a little liqueur
on hand, and plain
or honeyed yogurt to
pour over

Hot Watercress Soup

* * *

Crusty Aubergine and
plain bulgur wheat
with a salad of chopped
hard-boiled eggs, watercress,
cucumber and walnuts, with
Blue Cheese Dressing

* * *

Pashka (Russian cheesecake)

These dishes can be made in advance, or in the case of soup, made and reheated just before they are wanted.

Unexpected guests

Feeding the 5,000 without warning is a true test of the cook-in-a-hurry. Here are some useful ideas for what are usually informal meals:

For children
Fishburgers, followed by Baked Apples or Raisin and Apple Pancakes
or
Cheese and Oat Burgers, followed by Grilled Bananas
or
Not-just-stodge Pizza, followed by Fruit Salad

For a Crowd
Not-just-stodge Pizza with a salad; then stewed rhubarb or apples, both with raisins and honey
or
Fish Chowder — with wholemeal bread; then a big mixed salad with cheese
or
Spaghetti 'Marinara', with green salad; then Hot Spiced Fruit Salad

For People You Wish to Impress
Stuffed Tomatoes, then Spanish Omelette, then Hot Spiced Fruit Salad
or
Tjatjiki, then Savoury Swiss Roll with vegetables, then Oat and Honey Grapefruit
or
Peanut Patties, with green salad or vegetables, then Whole-meal Muesli, made with extra fresh fruit

INDEX